Sounds
and
Silences

HAYDEN SERIES IN LITERATURE

Robert W. Boynton, Consulting Editor

*Former Principal, Senior High School
and Chairman, English Department
Germantown Friends School*

Sounds
and
Silences

Poems for Performing

ROBERT W. BOYNTON

and

MAYNARD MACK

Yale University

HAYDEN BOOK COMPANY, INC.

Rochelle Park, New Jersey

Acknowledgments

SAMUEL ALLEN. "A Moment Please" reprinted by permission of the author.

W. H. AUDEN. "O What Is that Sound?" Copyright 1937 and renewed 1965 by W. H. Auden. Reprinted from *Collected Shorter Poems 1927–1957,* by W. H. Auden, by permission of Random House, Inc.

JOHN BETJEMAN. "The Licorice Fields at Pontefract" and "Winter Seascape." From *Collected Poems* by John Betjeman, reprinted by permission of John Murray (Publishers) Inc. and Houghton Mifflin Co.

GWENDOLYN BROOKS. "We Real Cool" from *The World of Gwendolyn Brooks* by Gwendolyn Brooks. Copyright © 1959 by Gwendolyn Brooks. Reprinted by permission of Harper & Row, Publishers, Inc.

JOHN CIARDI. "Chorus," from *As If* by John Ciardi. Reprinted by permission of the author.

COUNTEE CULLEN. "Yet Do I Marvel" from *On These I Stand* by Countee Cullen. Copyright 1925 by Harper & Row, Publishers, Inc.; renewed 1953 by Ida M. Cullen. Reprinted by permission of the publisher.

WALTER DE LA MARE. "The Listeners" and "Silver" from *The Complete Poems of Walter de la Mare 1970.* Reprinted by permission of The Literary Trustees of Walter de la Mare, and the Society of Authors as their representative.

WILLIAM DICKEY. "Exploration over the Rim" from *Of the Festivity,* Yale University Press, 1959. Copyright 1971 by William Dickey and used with his permission.

EMILY DICKINSON. "I'm Nobody. Who Are You?," "Much Madness Is Divinest Sense," and "The Snow." Reprinted by permission of the publishers and the Trustees of Amherst College, from Thomas H. Johnson, Editor, *The Poems of Emily Dickinson,* Cambridge,

Library of Congress Cataloging in Publication Data

Boynton, Robert W. comp.
  Sounds and silences.

  (Hayden series in literature)
  SUMMARY: Seventy-four poems selected for reading aloud with question-commentaries that suggest ways of performing each one.
  1. English poetry. 2. American poetry. 3. Oral interpretation—Juvenile literature. [1. Poetry—Collections. 2. Oral interpretation] I. Mack, Maynard joint comp. II. Title.
PR1175.B68   821'.9'1408   74-34215
ISBN 0-8104-5501-3

1   2   3   4   5   6   7   8   9   PRINTING

75 76 77 78 79 80 81 82   YEAR

Preface

Poetry is first and foremost a performer's art. Its life is in the spoken language, in the application of normal speech sounds and rhythms to gain varied and subtle ends. To enjoy it you must speak and hear it—either out loud or in your head—and this is, fortunately, a skill that can be learned.

We have called this book *Sounds and Silences: Poems for Performing* because we feel that the best way to develop that skill is to treat poems as performances—to read aloud over and over, trying different emphases, playing with different phrasing, letting the rhythms echo in the head, and so getting to know a number of poems so well they'll never be forgotten.

Like singing in the shower, performing a poem requires only a self-audience—and the pleasure is infinitely repeatable. Unlike singing in the shower, added pleasure comes from reading or reciting in front of an audience, either a handful at home or several handsful in the classroom. Whichever way, the important thing is to get some poems into your verbal memory—singing around in your head like favorite tunes—and the more the better. Then you will never be alone.

Contents

Sounds
and
Silences

Introduction

If you play a musical instrument or sing in some sort of choral group, you know the repeated pleasure that comes from having a piece so much at your command that you find yourself refining your performance of it every time you go through it. Actors don't grow tired of a good part, even if they play it night after night and twice on Wednesdays and Saturdays. The basketball player who has perfected a jump shot could throw it up all day without getting bored. The same thing, over and over again.

But is it the same thing? Each performer would hedge on the question: "In a sense it's the same thing, but only in the most superficial way. It may seem monotonously similar to anyone watching, but to me it's different every time I do it. I've got it under control—could do it in my sleep—but that's when I like it most: when I don't have to think about what I'm doing, when I can just enjoy doing it well and even fool around with it because I know I have it under control."

There are thousands of skills that various people are expert enough in to enjoy in the way we're talking about, and *reading* poetry—aloud or silently—is one of them. The demands it makes on a reader to do more with it than find out its literal sense require practice, repeated performance, familiarity, ease—all the qualities that make skills ultimately enjoyable. Nobody plays the piano well or makes jump shots consistently without a lot of practice and without the early frustration of being a bungler. The problem is to get past the stage of feeling strange and inept—the temptation to say that the pleasure in doing something well is not worth the time and effort it demands. If you do with this book what we suggest that you do, we think you'll avoid that temptation with respect to poetry, even if not with respect to jump shots.

1

The format of the book is simple, and dealing with it should be painless. It is divided into three parts. The first has 25 short poems in a variety of forms, moods, subjects, and idioms. The second has 49 poems of varying length gathered into seven groups. The third offers question-commentaries on each poem.

In selecting the poems we've been guided by two considerations:

(1) We've picked poems that read easily. That doesn't mean that they are immediately understood or that they are simple-minded, but that they have an instantly recognizable rhythmic flow, a "music" that grabs in an intriguing way, a pleasing regularity of language form that almost invites us not to worry about whether we understand what they "say." It's foolish to argue that it doesn't make any difference what a poem "says"—after all, language is meant to convey meaning as well as make a noise—but it's just as foolish to worry a poem to a frazzle to get all its "meaning" out. There is decided delight in the sound of words that sing together, and many a poem complex in meaning can delight even very young children with its verbal music—though they may make little "sense" of it.

(2) We've also picked some of the acknowledged finest poems in the language, written over a spread of several centuries. We're not pushing for "appreciation of the classics"; our feeling is simply that those we have chosen will hit you where you live. If in the process of becoming familiar with them you also become familiar with some of the great poets of the world, that's a free dividend.

Part I   The 25 poems in the first part are all short, all printed on separate pages. What we ask you to do is to read them through several times (in class over a period or two or at home over a day or two)—preferably, the first time, in the order in which they appear —keeping track of those you find most appealing. Don't spend time puzzling over unusual words or phrasing, and be sure to ignore the question-commentaries at the back of the book, unless you're the kind who opens packages labeled "Do Not Open Before Christmas" as soon as you see the label.

After you've read the first group of poems several times, take a look at the question-commentaries in Part III. We've called them "Ways In" because that's what they're meant to be—not questions looking for answers, but rather suggestions of possible interpretations that may not have occurred to you, or indications of double meanings and unusual uses of words or phrases. Our purpose is not to read the poem for you, a mistake we think many books of this kind make, but simply to provide the finger exercises that will make it easier for you to do that yourself.

Once you've become reasonably familiar with each of the poems, settle on three or four that you happen especially to like and read them over and over—preferably out loud if you can find a private place. Next, find an audience (your parents or some friends) and *perform* them. Keep the text in front of you, but occasionally try going for several lines without looking at it—as you would have to do if you were taking on a role in a play. Whatever you do, don't "recite" the poems; simply *speak* them, bearing in mind the group listening: what do you want them to feel? to understand? what needs emphasis and how? what kind of response are they making to you? (look at them occasionally).

Repeat this process a few times and you'll find that the poems have become so familiar that you'll be able to speak them from memory, even though you haven't consciously "memorized" them. Keep speaking them—several times a day—out loud or to yourself —and you'll find further that they don't grow stale, that you continually uncover new shades of meaning. Throughout the school year return often to the Part I poems and add one or two each time to your *knowing* list in the same way that you internalized the first three or four.

Part II   The second part is divided into seven groups of seven poems each, for no particular reason. The headings of the groups are self-explanatory, and some of the questions suggest why they are bunched as they are. No piece of literature needs another by its side or at its back to help define or enlarge its meaning, but it makes for curiosity and pleasure to compare quite different treatments of a similar idea. You may think that we have bundled some strange bedfellows. To say why you think so, and why we didn't think so, is a valuable finger exercise in itself.

Part III   For each poem (except the final seven) we have included some question-commentaries that are meant to suggest ways of speaking or performing it. Again, they are not meant to read the poem for you, but only to light up some corners where interesting meanings lurk. Be sure to give every poem a good oral workout—first aloud to yourself, then aloud to small groups (even a small group of one plus yourself), and then—individually or perhaps in choral form, with some passages performed by individual members of the chorus, some by the whole group of four to six speaking collectively as one— to an entire class or even school. By that time, you won't need us to tell you that reading poetry well has as many satisfactions as making jump shots or playing the piano well. The point, of course, is not to give up one for the other, but to enjoy both.

PART
I

25 Short Poems

1

The Young Ones, Flip Side

In tight pants, tight skirts,
stretched or squeezed,
youth hurts.
Crammed in, bursting out,
Flesh will sing
And hide its doubt
In nervous hips, hopping glance,
Usurping rouge,
Provoking stance.

Put off, or put on,
Youth hurts. And then
It's gone.

James A. Emanuel (1921–   )

A Question-Commentary for this poem will be found on pg. 89.

2

I'm Nobody. Who Are You?

I'm nobody. Who are you?
Are you nobody too?
Then there's a pair of us.
Don't tell—they'd banish us, you know.

5   How dreary to be somebody,
How public—like a frog—
To tell your name the livelong June
To an admiring bog.

Emily Dickinson (1830–1886)

A Question-Commentary for this poem will be found on pg. 89.

3

Dust of Snow

The way a crow
Shook down on me
The dust of snow
From a hemlock tree

5   Has given my heart
A change of mood
And saved some part
Of a day I had rued.°

Robert Frost (1874–1963)

A Question-Commentary for this poem will be found on pg. 90.

° *rued:*   regretted (that is, wished had never dawned)

4

Résumé

Razors pain you;
Rivers are damp;
Acids stain you;
And drugs cause cramp.
5   Guns aren't lawful;
Nooses give;
Gas smells awful;
You might as well live.

Dorothy Parker (1893–1967)

A Question-Commentary for this poem will be found on pg. 90.

5

The Clod and the Pebble

"Love secketh not itself to please,
    Nor for itself hath any care,
But for another gives its ease,
    And builds a heaven in hell's despair."

5   So sung a little clod of clay,
    Trodden with the cattle's feet,
But a pebble of the brook
    Warbled out these meters meet ° :

"Love seeketh only self to please,
10   To bind another to its delight,
Joys in another's loss of ease,
    And builds a hell in heaven's despite." °

William Blake (1757–1827)

A Question-Commentary for this poem will be found on pg. 91.

° *meet :*   fitting, proper
° *despite:*   malice, contempt

6

The Amish °

The Amish are a surly sect.
They paint their bulging barns with hex
Designs, pronounce a dialect
Of Deutsch,° inbreed, and wink at sex.

5   They have no use for buttons, tea,
Life insurance, cigarettes,
Churches, liquor, Sea & Ski,
Public power, or regrets.

Believing motors undivine,
10   They bob behind a buggied horse
From Paradise to Brandywine,
From Bird-in-Hand to Intercourse.°

They think the Devil drives a car
And wish Jehovah would revoke
15   The licensed fools who travel far
To gaze upon these simple folk.

John Updike (1932–   )

A Question-Commentary for this poem will be found on pg. 91.

° *Amish:* a religious sect (Mennonite Christian) stressing simple living
° *Deutsch:* German (often misleadingly called Dutch, as in Pennsylvania Dutch)
° *Paradise . . . Intercourse:* towns in eastern Pennsylvania (Amish country)

7

Esthete in Harlem

Strange,
That in this nigger place
I should meet life face to face;
When, for years, I had been seeking
Life in places gentler-speaking,
Until I came to this vile street
And found Life stepping on my feet!

Langston Hughes (1902–1967)

A Question-Commentary for this poem will be found on pg. 91.

8

A Choice of Weapons

Sticks and stones are hard on bones.
Aimed with angry art,
Words can sting like anything.
But silence breaks the heart.

Phyllis McGinley (1905–   )

A Question-Commentary for this poem will be found on pg. 92.

9

Which Is My Little Boy

Which is my little boy, which is he,
Jean qui pleure ° *ou Jean qui rit?* °

Jean qui rit is my delicate John,
the one with the Chinese slippers on,

5   whose hobbyhorse in a single bound
carries me back to native ground.

But *Jean qui pleure* is *mysterieux* °
with sorrows older than Naishapur,°

with all of the stars and all of the moons
10   mirrored in little silver spoons.

Which is my little boy, which is he,
Jean qui pleure ou Jean qui rit?

Tennessee Williams (1914–   )

A Question-Commentary for this poem will be found on pg. 92.

° *Jean qui pleure:*   John who cries
° *ou Jean qui rit:*   or John who laughs
° *mysterieux:*   full of mystery
° *Naishapur:*   ancient Persian city

10

The End of the World

Quite unexpectedly as Vasserot
The armless ambidextrian was lighting
A match between his great and second toe
And Ralph the lion was engaged in biting
5   The neck of Madame Sossman while the drum
Pointed,° and Teeny was about to cough
In waltz time swinging Jocko by the thumb—
Quite unexpectedly the top blew off:

And there, there overhead, there, there, hung over
10   Those thousands of white faces, those dazed eyes,
There in the starless dark the poise, the hover,
There with vast wings across the canceled skies,
There in the sudden blackness the black pall
Of nothing, nothing, nothing—nothing at all.

Archibald MacLeish (1892–   )

A Question-Commentary for this poem will be found on pg. 93.

° *Pointed:*   rolled (beat rapidly)

11

The Sloth

In moving-slow he has no Peer.
You ask him something in his Ear,
He thinks about it for a Year;

And, then, before he says a Word
There, upside down (unlike a Bird),
He will assume that you have Heard—

A most Ex-as-per-at-ing Lug.
But should you call his manner Smug,
He'll sigh and give his Branch a Hug;

Then off again to Sleep he goes,
Still swaying gently by his Toes,
And you just *know* he knows he knows.

Theodore Roethke (1908–1963)

A Question-Commentary for this poem will be found on pg. 93.

12

The Garden of Love

I went to the Garden of Love
And I saw what I never had seen:
A Chapel was built in the midst,
Where I used to play on the green.

5   And the gates of this Chapel were shut,
And "Thou shalt not" writ over the door;
So I turned to the Garden of Love
That so many sweet flowers bore;

And I saw it was filled with graves,
10   And tomb-stones where flowers should be;
And Priests in black gowns were walking their rounds,
And binding with briars my joys and desires.

William Blake (1757–1827)

A Question-Commentary for this poem will be found on pg. 94.

---

archy confesses

coarse
jocosity
catches the crowd
shakespeare
5   and i
are often
low browed

the fish wife
curse
10   and the laugh
of the horse
shakespeare
and i
are frequently
15   coarse

aesthetic
excuses
in bill s behalf
are adduced
20   to refine
big bill s
coarse laugh

but bill
he would chuckle
25   to hear such guff
he pulled
rough stuff
and he liked
rough stuff

30   hoping you
are the same
          archy

Don Marquis (1878–1937)

A Question-Commentary for this poem will be found on pg. 94.

14

Much Madness Is Divinest Sense

Much madness is divinest sense
To a discerning eye—
Much sense the starkest madness.
'Tis the majority
5   In this, as all, prevail.
Assent and you are sane;
Demur,° you're straightway dangerous
And handled with a chain.

Emily Dickinson (1830–1886)

A Question-Commentary for this poem will be found on pg. 94.

° *demur:*   object

15

The Eagle

He clasps the crag with crooked hands;
Close to the sun in lonely lands,
Ringed with the azure world, he stands.

The wrinkled sea beneath him crawls;
5   He watches from his mountain walls,
And like a thunderbolt he falls.

Alfred, Lord Tennyson (1809–1892)

A Question-Commentary for this poem will be found on pg. 95.

16

Upon Julia's Clothes

Whenas ° in silks my Julia goes,
Then, then, methinks, how sweetly flows
That liquefaction ° of her clothes.

Next, when I cast mine eyes and see
5   That brave ° vibration each way free,
Oh, how that glittering taketh me!

Robert Herrick (1591–1674)

A Question-Commentary for this poem will be found on pg. 95.

° *Whenas:*   when
° *liquefaction:*   having a liquid-like quality
° *brave:*   bright and splendid

17

The Debt

This is the debt I pay
Just for one riotous day,
Years of regret and grief,
Sorrow without relief.

5   Pay it I will to the end—
Until the grave, my friend,
Gives me a true release—
Gives me the clasp of peace.

Slight was the thing I bought,
10   Small was the debt I thought,
Poor was the loan at best—
God! but the interest!

Paul Laurence Dunbar (1872–1906)

A Question-Commentary for this poem will be found on pg. 95.

18

The Pennycandystore Beyond the El °

The pennycandystore beyond the El
is where I first
       fell in love
           with unreality
Jellybeans glowed in the semi-gloom
of that september afternoon
A cat upon the counter moved among
              the licorice sticks
      and tootsie rolls
      and Oh Boy Gum

Outside the leaves were falling as they died

A wind had blown away the sun

A girl ran in
Her hair was rainy
Her breasts were breathless in the little room

Outside the leaves were falling
       and they cried
           Too soon! too soon!

Lawrence Ferlinghetti (1919–   )

A Question-Commentary for this poem will be found on pg. 96.

° *El :*   elevated railway

19

Eldorado °

Gaily bedight,°
A gallant knight,
In sunshine and in shadow,
Had journeyed long,
Singing a song,
In search of Eldorado.

But he grew old—
This knight so bold—
And o'er his heart a shadow
Fell as he found
No spot of ground
That looked like Eldorado.

And, as his strength
Failed him at length,
He met a pilgrim shadow—
"Shadow," said he,
"Where can it be—
This land of Eldorado?"

"Over the mountains
Of the moon,
Down the valley of the shadow,
Ride, boldly ride,"
The shade replied,—
"If you seek for Eldorado!"

Edgar Allan Poe (1809–1849)

A Question-Commentary for this poem will be found on pg. 96.

° *Eldorado:*   a mythical land of great riches; hence anything greatly desirable
° *bedight:*   dressed, adorned

20

Silver

Slowly, silently, now the moon
Walks the night in her silver shoon;
This way, and that, she peers, and sees
Silver fruit upon silver trees;
5   One by one the casements catch
Her beams beneath the silvery thatch;
Couched in his kennel, like a log,
With paws of silver sleeps the dog;
From their shadowy cote the white breasts peep
10   Of doves in a silver-feathered sleep;
A harvest mouse goes scampering by,
With silver claws, and a silver eye;
And moveless fish in the water gleam,
By silver reeds in a silver stream.

Walter de la Mare (1873–1956)

A Question-Commentary for this poem will be found on pg. 96.

21

They Told Me You Had Been to Her

"Begin at the beginning," the King said gravely, "and go on till you come to the end; then stop."

These were the verses the White Rabbit read:

"They told me you had been to her,
And mentioned me to him:
She gave me a good character,
But said I could not swim.

5   He sent them word I had not gone
(We know it to be true):
If she should push the matter on,
What would become of you?

I gave her one, they gave him two,
10   You gave us three or more;
They all returned from him to you,
Though they were mine before.

If I or she should chance to be
Involved in this affair,
15   He trusts to you to set them free,
Exactly as we were.

My notion was that you had been
(Before she had this fit)
An obstacle that came between
20   Him, and ourselves, and it.

Don't let him know she liked them best,
For this must ever be
A secret, kept from all the rest,
Between yourself and me."

Lewis Carroll (1832–1898)

A Question-Commentary for this poem will be found on pg. 97.

22

Girl's Song

I went out alone
To sing a song or two,
My fancy on a man,
And you know who.

5   Another came in sight
That on a stick relied
To hold himself upright;
I sat and cried.

And that was all my song—
10   When everything is told,
Saw I an old man young
Or young man old?

William Butler Yeats (1865–1939)

A Question-Commentary for this poem will be found on pg. 97.

We Real Cool

The Pool Players.
Seven at the Golden Shovel.

We real cool. We
Left school. We

Lurk late. We
Strike straight. We

5   Sing sin. We
Thin gin. We

Jazz June. We
Die soon.

Gwendolyn Brooks (1917–   )

A Question-Commentary for this poem will be found on pg. 97.

24

This Is Just to Say

I have eaten
the plums
that were in
the icebox

5   and which
you were probably
saving
for breakfast

Forgive me
10   they were delicious
so sweet
and so cold

William Carlos Williams (1883–1963)

A Question-Commentary for this poem will be found on pg. 98.

Not Waving But Drowning

Nobody heard him, the dead man,
But still he lay moaning:
I was much further out than you thought
And not waving but drowning.

5   Poor chap, he always loved larking °
And now he's dead
It must have been too cold for him his heart gave way,
They said.

Oh, no no no, it was too cold always
10   (Still the dead one lay moaning)
I was much too far out all my life
And not waving but drowning.

Stevie Smith (1902–1971)

A Question-Commentary for this poem will be found on pg. 98.

° *larking:* fooling around

PART
II

49 More Poems

in Seven Groups of Seven

1

SOME PLANNED AND
UNPLANNED ENDINGS

1ᵃ

Chorus

They were singing Old MacDonald in the schoolbus
With a *peep peep* here and a *peep peep* there after
Margie Littenach had been delivered to the right mailbox
And the gears had gnashed their teeth uphill to the Cliff
    House
Where the driver, shifting gears, honked at the
        countergirls,
And the tourists turned from panorama all smiles
To remember schooldays, long curls, hooky, and how
The view had always stretched for miles and miles
Where the gentle cumulus puffed small in gentle weather
Putting a cottonfluff roof on the green world leaning
    down hill
To the bluelevelfield of sea, and all together
With an *oink oink* here and a *moo moo* there the children
Were singing Old MacDonald in the schoolbus

When a bolt fell from the compound interest problem,
A rod broke in the third chapter of the Civicsbook
Where the county had no money for inspection in the
    first place
                and
Momentum had no brakes, but with a *honk honk* here
And a *honk honk* there went sidewise over tirescreech
Downturning in round air away from panorama where
Even the tourists could tell sea didn't measure each
Stone falling, or button, or bolt, or Caroline Helmhold,
Nor anywhere its multitudinous self incarnadine, but
    only swallowed

What books, belts, lunchpails, pity
25   Spilled over the touristfaredge of the world and Old
     MacDonald

John Ciardi (1916–   )

A Question-Commentary for this poem will be found on pg. 99.

1^b

A Moment Please

When I gaze at the sun
    I walked to the subway booth
    for change for a dime.
and know that this great earth
5   Two adolescent girls stood there
    alive with eagerness to know
is but a fragment from it thrown
    all in their new found world
    there was for them to know
10 *in heat and flame a billion years ago,*
    they looked at me and brightly asked
    "Are you Arabian?"
that then this world was lifeless
    I smiled and cautiously
15   —for one grows cautious—
    shook my head.
as, a billion hence,
    "Egyptian?"
it shall again be,
20   Again I smiled and shook my head
    and walked away.
what moment is it that I am betrayed,
    I've gone but seven paces now
oppressed, cast down,
25   and from behind comes swift the sneer
or warm with love or triumph?
    "Or Nigger?"

    A moment, please
What is it that to fury I am roused?

30 for still it takes a moment
What meaning for me
and now
in this homeless clan
I'll turn
35 *the dupe of space*
and smile
the toy of time?
and nod my head.

Samuel Allen (1917–   )

A Question-Commentary for this poem will be found on pg. 100.

1^c

Song

The stranger lighted from his steed,
    And ere he spake a word,
He seiz'd my lady's lily hand,
    And kiss'd it all unheard.

5 The stranger walk'd into the hall,
    And ere he spake a word,
He kiss'd my lady's cherry lips,
    And kiss'd 'em all unheard.

The stranger walk'd into the bower,—
10   But my lady first did go,—
Aye hand in hand into the bower,
    Where my lord's roses blow.

My lady's maid had a silken scarf,
    And a golden ring had she,
15 And a kiss from the stranger, as off he went
    Again on his fair palfrey.°

John Keats (1795–1821)

A Question-Commentary for this poem will be found on pg. 100.

° *palfrey:* a seldom used word for a horse

1^d

Vale° *from Carthage*

(in memory of my brother, an American corporal
shot at Rome by the Nazis in spring, 1944)

I, now at Carthage. He, shot dead at Rome.
Shipmates last May. "And what if one of us,"
I asked last May, in fun, in gentleness,
"Wears doom, like dungarees, and doesn't know?"
5   He laughed, *"Not see Times Square again?"* The foam,
Feathering across that deck a year ago,
Swept those five words—like seeds—beyond the seas
    Into his future. There they grew like trees;
    And as he passed them there next spring, they laid
10   Upon his road of fire their sudden shade.
Though he had always scraped his mess-kit pure
And scrubbed redeemingly his barracks floor,
Though all his buttons glowed their ritual-hymn
Like cloudless moons to intercede for him,
15   No furlough fluttered from the sky. He will
Not see Times Square—he will not see—he will
Not see Times
              change; at Carthage (while my friend,
Living those words at Rome, screamed in the end)
20   I saw an ancient Roman's tomb and read
"Vale" in stone. Here two wars mix their dead:
    Roman, my shipmate's dream walks hand in hand
    With yours tonight ("New York again" and
        "Rome"),
    Like widowed sisters bearing water home
25   On tired heads through hot Tunisian sand
    In good cool urns, and says, "I understand."
Roman, you'll see your Forum Square no more;
What's left but this to say of any war?

Peter Viereck (1916–   )

A Question-Commentary for this poem will be found on pg. 100.

° *Vale:*   farewell

1ᵉ

Meeting at Night

The gray sea and the long black land;
And the yellow half-moon large and low;
And the startled little waves that leap
In fiery ringlets from their sleep,
As I gain the cove with pushing prow,
And quench its speed i' the slushy sand.

Then a mile of warm sea-scented beach;
Three fields to cross till a farm appears;
A tap at the pane, the quick sharp scratch
And blue spurt of a lighted match,
And a voice less loud, through its joys and fears,
Than the two hearts beating each to each!

Robert Browning (1812–1889)

A Question-Commentary for this poem will be found on pg. 101.

1ᶠ

Exploration over the Rim

Beyond that sandbar is the river's turning.
There a new country opens up to sight,
Safe from the fond researches of our learning.
Here it is day; there it is always night.

Around this corner is a certain danger.
The streets are streets of hell from here on in.
The Anthropophagi ° and beings stranger
Roast in the fire and meditate on sin.

After this kiss will I know who I'm kissing?
Will I have reached the point of no return?
What happened to those others who are missing?
Oh, well, to hell with it. If we burn, we burn.

William Dickey (1928–   )

A Question-Commentary for this poem will be found on pg. 101.

° *Anthropophagi:* cannibals

Molly Means

Old Molly Means was a hag and a witch;
Chile of the devil, the dark, and sitch.
Her heavy hair hung thick in ropes
And her blazing eyes was black as pitch.
5 Imp at three and wench at 'leben
She counted her husbands to the number seben.
    O Molly, Molly, Molly Means
    There goes the ghost of Molly Means.

Some say she was born with a veil on her face
10 So she could look through unnatchal space
Through the future and through the past
And charm a body or an evil place
And every man could well despise
The evil look in her coal black eyes.
15   Old Molly, Molly, Molly Means
    Dark is the ghost of Molly Means.

And when the tale begun to spread
Of evil and of holy dread:
Her black-hand arts and her evil powers
20 How she cast her spells and called the dead,
The younguns was afraid at night
And the farmers feared their crops would blight.
    Old Molly, Molly, Molly Means
    Cold is the ghost of Molly Means.

25 Then one dark day she put a spell
On a young gal-bride just come to dwell
In the lane just down from Molly's shack
And when her husband come riding back
His wife was barking like a dog
30 And on all fours like a common hog.
    O Molly, Molly, Molly Means
    Where is the ghost of Molly Means?

The neighbors come and they went away
And said she'd die before break of day
35 But her husband held her in his arms
And swore he'd break the wicked charms;

He'd search all up and down the land
And turn the spell on Molly's hand.
    O Molly, Molly, Molly Means
40   Sharp is the ghost of Molly Means.

So he rode all day and he rode all night
And at the dawn he come in sight
Of a man who said he could move the spell
And cause the awful thing to dwell
45 On Molly Means, to bark and bleed
Till she died at the hands of her evil deed.
    Old Molly, Molly, Molly Means
    This is the ghost of Molly Means.

Sometimes at night through the shadowy trees
50 She rides along on a winter breeze.
You can hear her holler and whine and cry.
Her voice is thin and her moan is high,
And her cackling laugh or her barking cold
Bring terror to the young and old.
55   O Molly, Molly, Molly Means
    Lean is the ghost of Molly Means.

Margaret Walker (1915–   )

A Question-Commentary for this poem will be found on pg. 101.

SOME SWEET AND SOUR
LOVE NOTES

2ᵃ

Launcelot with Bicycle

Her window looks upon the lane.
From it, anonymous and shy,
Twice daily she can see him plain,
Wheeling heroic by.
5 She droops her cheek against the pane
And gives a little sigh.

Above him maples at their bloom
Shake April pollen down like stars
While he goes whistling past her room
10 Toward unimagined wars,
A tennis visor for his plume,
Scornful of handlebars.

And, counting over in her mind
His favors, gleaned like windfall fruit
15 (A morning when he spoke her kind,
An afterschool salute,
A number that she helped him find,
Once, for his paper route),

Sadly she twists a stubby braid
20 And closer to the casement leans—
A wistful and a lily maid
In moccasins and jeans,
Despairing from the seventh grade
To match his lordly teens.

25 And so she grieves in Astolat
(Where other girls have grieved the same)

For being young and therefore not
Sufficient to his fame—
Who will by summer have forgot
30   Grief, April, and his name.

Phyllis McGinley (1905–   )

A Question-Commentary for this poem will be found on pg. 102.

2^b

Vain Gratuities

Never was there a man much uglier
In eyes of other women, or more grim:
"The Lord has filled her chalice to the brim,
So let us pray she's a philosopher,"
5   They said; and there was more they said of her—
Deeming it, after twenty years with him,
No wonder that she kept her figure slim
And always made you think of lavender.

But she, demure as ever, and as fair,
10   Almost, as they remembered her before
She found him, would have laughed had she been there;
And all they said would have been heard no more
Than foam that washes on an island shore
Where there are none to listen or to care.

Edwin Arlington Robinson (1869–1935)

A Question-Commentary for this poem will be found on pg. 102.

2^c

Green Grow the Rashes

Green grow the rashes ° O,
    Green grow the rashes O;
The sweetest hours that e'er I spend,
    Are spent amang the lasses O!

° *rashes:* rushes

---

5 There's nought but care on ev'ry han',
     In ev'ry hour that passes O;
What signifies the life o' man,
     An' ° 'twere na for the lasses O.

The warly ° race may riches chase,
10   An' riches still may fly them O;
An' tho' at last they catch them fast,
     Their hearts can ne'er enjoy them O.

But gie ° me a canny ° hour at e'en
     My arms about my dearie O;
15 An' warly cares, an' warly men,
     May a' ° gae ° tapsalteerie ° O!

For you sae °douce,° ye sneer at this,
     Ye're nought but senseless asses O:
The wisest man ° the warl' e'er saw,
20   He dearly lov'd the lasses O.

Auld nature swears, the lovely dears
     Her noblest work she classes O;
Her prentice ° han' she tried on man,
     An' then she made the lasses O.

Robert Burns (1759–1796)

A Question-Commentary for this poem will be found on pg. 102.

2^d

Barbara Allan

It was in and about the Martinmas time,
     When the green leaves were a falling,
That Sir John Graeme, in the West Country,
     Fell in love with Barbara Allan.

° *An'*: and (meaning here "if")	° *tapsalteerie*: topsy-turvy
° *warly*: wordly	° *sae*: so
° *canny*: quiet	° *douce*: solemn, sober
° *a'*: all	° *wisest man*: Solomon
° *gae*: go	° *prentice*: apprentice

He sent his man down through the town,
  To the place where she was dwelling:
"O haste and come to my master dear,
  Gin ° ye be Barbara Allan."

O hooly,° hooly rose she up,
  To the place where he was lying,
And when she drew the curtain by,
  "Young man, I think you're dying."

"O it's I'm sick, and very, very sick,
  And 't is a' for Barbara Allan:"
"O the better for me ye's never be,
  Tho your heart's blood were a spilling.

"O dinna ye mind,° young man," said she,
  "When ye was in the tavern a drinking,
That ye made the healths gae round and round,
  And slighted Barbara Allan?"

He turnd his face unto the wall,
  And death was with him dealing:
"Adieu, adieu, my dear friends all,
  And be kind to Barbara Allan."

And slowly, slowly raise she up,
  And slowly, slowly left him,
And sighing said, she coud not stay,
  Since death of life had reft ° him,

She had not gane a mile but twa,
  When she heard the dead-bell ringing,
And every jow ° that the dead-bell gied,°
  It cry'd, Woe to Barbara Allan!

"O mother, mother, make my bed!
  O make it saft and narrow!
Since my love died for me to-day,
  I'll die for him to-morrow."

Anonymous

A Question-Commentary for this poem will be found on pg. 103.

° *Gin:*	if	° *reft:*	robbed
° *hooly:*	softly	° *jow:*	toll
° *mind:*	remember	° *gied:*	gave

For Hettie

My wife is left-handed.
which implies a fierce de-
termination. A complete other
worldliness. ITS WEIRD, BABY.
5 The way some folks
are always trying to be
different. A sin & a shame.

But then, she's been a bohemian
all of her life . . . black stockings
10 refusing to take orders. I sit
patiently, trying to tell her
whats right. TAKE THAT DAMM
PENCIL OUTTA THAT HAND. YOU'RE
RITING BACKWARDS. & such. But
15 to no avail. & it shows
in her work. Left-handed coffee,
Left-handed eggs; when she comes
in at night . . . it's her left hand
offered for me to kiss. Damm.
20 & now her belly droops over the seat.
They say it's a child. But
I ain't quite so sure.

LeRoi Jones (1934–   )

A Question-Commentary for this poem will be found on pg. 103.

The Licorice Fields at Pontefract °

In the licorice fields at Pontefract
  My love and I did meet
And many a burdened licorice bush
  Was blooming round our feet;
5 Red hair she had and golden skin,

° *Pontefract:* town in Yorkshire, England

Her sulky lips were shaped for sin,
Her sturdy legs were flannel-slack'd,
The strongest legs in Pontefract.

The light and dangling licorice flowers
    Gave off the sweetest smells;
From various black Victorian towers
    The Sunday evening bells
Came pealing over dales and hills
And tanneries and silent mills
And lowly streets where country stops
And little shuttered corner shops.

She cast her blazing eyes on me
    And plucked a licorice leaf;
I was her captive slave and she
    My red-haired robber chief.
Oh love! for love I could not speak,
It left me winded, wilting, weak
And held in brown arms strong and bare
And wound with flaming ropes of hair.

John Betjeman (1916–   )

A Question-Commentary for this poem will be found on pg. 103.

2^g

Neutral Tones

We stood by a pond that winter day,
And the sun was white as though chidden of ° God,
And a few leaves lay on the starving sod;
    —They had fallen from an ash, and were gray.

Your eyes on me were as eyes that rove
Over tedious riddles solved years ago;
And some words played between us to and fro
    On which lost the more by our love.

° *chidden of :*   rebuked by

The smile on your mouth was the deadest thing
10   Alive enough to have strength to die;
And a grin of bitterness swept thereby
    Like an ominous bird a-wing. . . .

Since then, keen lessons that love deceives,
And wrings with wrong, have shaped to me
15   Your face, and the God-curst sun, and a tree,
    And a pond edged with grayish leaves.

Thomas Hardy (1840–1928)

A Question-Commentary for this poem will be found on pg. 104.

SOME QUESTIONS ASKED
AND ANSWERED

3ᵃ

Is My Team Ploughing

'Is my team ploughing,
    That I was used to drive
And hear the harness jingle
    When I was man alive?'

5   Ay, the horses trample,
    The harness jingles now;
No change though you lie under
    The land you used to plough.

'Is football playing
10   Along the river shore,
With lads to chase the leather,
    Now I stand up no more?'

Ay, the ball is flying,
    The lads play heart and soul;
15   The goal stands up, the keeper
    Stands up to keep the goal.

'Is my girl happy,
    That I thought hard to leave,
And has she tired of weeping
20   As she lies down at eve?'

Ay, she lies down lightly,
    She lies not down to weep:
Your girl is well contented.
    Be still, my lad, and sleep.

A. E. Housman (1859–1936)

A Question-Commentary for this poem will be found on pg. 104.

3^b

Dinner Guest: Me

I know I am
The Negro Problem
Being wined and dined,
Answering the usual questions
5 That come to white mind
Which seeks demurely
To probe in polite way
The why and wherewithal
Of darkness U.S.A.—
10 Wondering how things got this way
In current democratic night,
Murmuring gently
Over *fraises du bois*,°
"I'm so ashamed of being white."

15 The lobster is delicious,
The wine divine,
And center of attention
At the damask table, mine.
To be a Problem on
20 Park Avenue at eight
Is not so bad.
Solutions to the Problem,
Of course, wait.

Langston Hughes (1902–1967)

A Question-Commentary for this poem will be found on pg. 105.

3^c

The Listeners

"Is there anybody there?" said the Traveler,
Knocking on the moonlit door;
And his horse in the silence champed the grasses
Of the forest's ferny floor;
5 And a bird flew up out of the turret,

° *fraises du bois:* wild strawberries

Above the Traveler's head:
And he smote upon the door again a second time;
    "Is there anybody there?" he said.
But no one descended to the Traveler;
10   No head from the leaf-fringed sill
Leaned over and looked into his gray eyes,
    Where he stood perplexed and still.
But only a host of phantom listeners
    That dwelt in the lone house then
15   Stood listening in the quiet of the moonlight
    To that voice from the world of men:
Stood thronging the faint moonbeams on the dark stair,
    That goes down to the empty hall,
Hearkening in an air stirred and shaken
20   By the lonely Traveler's call.
And he felt in his heart their strangeness,
    Their stillness answering his cry,
While his horse moved, cropping the dark turf,
    'Neath the starred and leafy sky;
25   For he suddenly smote on the door, even
    Louder, and lifted his head:—
"Tell them I came, and no one answered,
    That I kept my word," he said.
Never the least stir made the listeners,
30   Though every word he spake
Fell echoing through the shadowiness of the still house
    From the one man left awake:
Ay, they heard his foot upon the stirrup,
    And the sound of iron on stone,
35   And how the silence surged softly backward,
    When the plunging hoofs were gone.

                     Walter de la Mare (1873–1956)

A Question-Commentary for this poem will be found on pg. 105.

3ᵈ

O What Is that Sound

O what is that sound which so thrills the ear
    Down in the valley drumming, drumming?
Only the scarlet soldiers, dear,
    The soldiers coming.

O what is that light I see flashing so clear
　　Over the distance brightly, brightly?
Only the sun on their weapons, dear,
　　As they step lightly.

O what are they doing with all that gear,
　　What are they doing this morning, this morning?
Only their usual manoeuvres, dear,
　　Or perhaps a warning.

O why have they left the road down there,
　　Why are they suddenly wheeling, wheeling?
Perhaps a change in their orders, dear.
　　Why are you kneeling?

O haven't they stopped for the doctor's care,
　　Haven't they reined their horses, their horses?
Why, they are none of them wounded, dear,
　　None of these forces.

O is it the parson they want, with white hair,
　　Is it the parson, is it, is it?
No, they are passing his gateway, dear,
　　Without a visit.

O it must be the farmer who lives so near.
　　It must be the farmer so cunning, so cunning?
They have passed the farmyard already, dear,
　　And now they are running.

O where are you going? Stay with me here!
　　Were the vows you swore deceiving, deceiving?
No, I promised to love you, dear,
　　But I must be leaving.

O it's broken the lock and splintered the door,
　　O it's the gate where they're turning, turning;
Their boots are heavy on the floor
　　And their eyes are burning.

W. H. Auden (1907–1973)

A Question-Commentary for this poem will be found on pg. 105.

Shall I Wasting in Despair

Shall I wasting in despair
Die because a woman's fair?
Or make pale my cheeks with care
'Cause another's rosy are?
5 Be she fairer than the day,
Or the flow'ry meads in May,
    If she be not so to me,
    What care I how fair she be?

Shall my heart be grieved or pined
10 'Cause I see a woman kind?
Or a well-disposèd nature
Joinèd with a lovely feature?
Be she meeker, kinder, than
Turtle-dove or pelican,
15   If she be not so to me,
    What care I how kind she be?

Shall a woman's virtues move
Me to perish for her love?
Or her well-deserving known
20 Make me quite forget mine own?
Be she with that goodness blest
Which may gain her name of best,
    If she be not such to me,
    What care I how good she be?

25 'Cause her fortune seems too high,
Shall I play the fool and die?
Those that bear a noble mind,
Where they want of riches find,
Think what with them they would do
30 That without them dare to woo;
    And unless that mind I see,
    What care I how great she be?

Great, or good, or kind, or fair,
I will ne'er the more despair;

If she love me, this believe,
I will die ere she shall grieve;
If she slight me when I woo,
I can scorn and let her go;
    For if she be not for me,
    What care I for whom she be?

George Wither (1588–1667)

A Question-Commentary for this poem will be found on pg. 105.

3^f

Up-Hill

Does the road wind up-hill all the way?
    Yes, to the very end.
Will the day's journey take the whole long day?
    From morn to night, my friend.

5   But is there for the night a resting-place?
    A roof for when the slow dark hours begin.
May not the darkness hide it from my face?
    You cannot miss that inn.

Shall I meet other wayfarers at night?
10   Those who have gone before.
Then must I knock, or call when just in sight?
    They will not keep you standing at that door.

Shall I find comfort, travel-sore and weak?
    Of labor you shall find the sum.
15   Will there be beds for me and all who seek?
    Yea, beds for all who come.

Christina Rossetti (1830–1894)

A Question-Commentary for this poem will be found on pg. 106.

Yet Do I Marvel

I doubt not God is good, well-meaning, kind.
And did He stoop to quibble could tell why
The little buried mole continues blind,
Why flesh that mirrors Him must some day die,
5   Make plain the reason tortured Tantalus
Is baited by the fickle fruit, declare
If merely brute caprice dooms Sisyphus
To struggle up a never-ending stair.
Inscrutable His ways are, and immune
10   To catechism ° by a mind too strewn
With petty cares to slightly understand
What awful brain compels His awful hand.
Yet do I marvel at this curious thing:
To make a poet black, and bid him sing!

Countee Cullen (1903–1946)

A Question-Commentary for this poem will be found on pg. 106.

° *catechism:*   a question-and-answer examination

4

SOME ADVICE FREELY GIVEN—
AND FREELY IGNORED

4ᵃ

When a Man Hath No Freedom
to Fight for at Home

When a man hath no freedom to fight for at home,
    Let him combat for that of his neighbors;
Let him think of the glories of Greece and of Rome,
    And get knocked on the head for his labors.

5   To do good to Mankind is the chivalrous plan,
    And is always as nobly requited; °
Then battle for freedom wherever you can,
    And, if not shot or hanged, you'll get knighted.

George Gordon, Lord Byron (1788–1824)

A Question-Commentary for this poem will be found on pg. 107.

4ᵇ

For Anne Gregory

'Never shall a young man,
Thrown into despair
By those great honey-colored
Ramparts at your ear,
5   Love you for yourself alone
And not your yellow hair.'

° *requited:*   paid back

'But I can get a hair-dye
And set such color there,
Brown, or black, or carrot,
10   That young men in despair
May love me for myself alone
And not my yellow hair.'

'I heard an old religious man
But yesternight declare
15   That he had found a text to prove
That only God, my dear,
Could love you for yourself alone
And not your yellow hair.'

William Butler Yeats (1865–1939)

A Question-Commentary for this poem will be found on pg. 107.

4^c

Provide, Provide

The witch that came (the withered hag)
To wash the steps with pail and rag
Was once the beauty Abishag,

The picture pride of Hollywood.
5   Too many fall from great and good
For you to doubt the likelihood.

Die early and avoid the fate.
Or if predestined to die late,
Make up your mind to die in state.

10   Make the whole stock exchange your own!
If need be occupy a throne,
Where nobody can call *you* crone.

Some have relied on what they knew,
Others on being simply true.
15   What worked for them might work for you.

No memory of having starred
Atones for later disregard
Or keeps the end from being hard.

Better to go down dignified
20   With boughten friendship at your side
Than none at all. Provide; provide!

Robert Frost (1874–1963)

A Question-Commentary for this poem will be found on pg. 107.

A Question-Commentary for this poem will be found on pg. 107.

4^d

Poetry of Departures

Sometimes you hear, fifth-hand,
As epitaph:
He chucked up everything
And just cleared off,
5   And always the voice will sound
Certain you approve
This audacious, purifying,
Elemental move.

And they are right, I think.
10   We all hate home
And having to be there:
I detest my room,
Its specially-chosen junk,
The good books, the good bed,
15   And my life, in perfect order:
So to hear it said

He walked out on the whole crowd
Leaves me flushed and stirred,
Like *Then she undid her dress*
20   Or *Take that you bastard;*
Surely I can, if he did?
And that helps me stay
Sober and industrious.
But I'd go today,

25 Yes, swagger the nut-strewn roads,
Crouch in the fo'c'sle
Stubbly with goodness, if
It weren't so artificial,
Such a deliberate step backwards
30 To create an object:
Books; china; a life
Reprehensibly perfect.

Philip Larkin (1922–   )

A Question-Commentary for this poem will be found on pg. 108.

4ᵉ

Underworld

You've seen coalminers coming up
for air, all in blackface like
no minstrel show comedian,
but bent over, seamed by the danger
5 and the darkness they must bear,
at once a badge and a wound.

Or maybe a diver on the deck,
his heavy helmet cast aside,
blinking in the hard bright light
10 where each breath is a gust of fire.
It is no laughing matter
to live in two strange worlds.

So it is with certain myths and dreams.
The songs of Orpheus never were the same
15 after he had seen hell. They roused
nothing but rage and madness; yet,
after such vision and total loss,
who wouldn't change his tune?

Oh, you will descend, all right,
20 dream into the fiery darkness or
stumble, awkward among the deep sea
shiftings, troubled by bones
and voiceless cries. And then
you wake and wonder what is real. . . .

25 Better to come back grinning,
scrub the darkness off yourself,
wisecrack with the ordinary seamen,
unless, like a careless saint,
you can give your soul to God.
30 And then your flesh belongs to furies.

George Garrett (1929–   )

A Question-Commentary for this poem will be found on pg. 108.

4^f

Blue Girls

Twirling your blue skirts, traveling the sward
Under the towers of your seminary,
Go listen to your teachers old and contrary
Without believing a word.

5 Tie the white fillets ° then about your hair
And think no more of what will come to pass
Than bluebirds that go walking on the grass
And chattering on the air.

Practice your beauty, blue girls, before it fail;
10 And I will cry with my loud lips and publish °
Beauty which all our power shall never establish,
It is so frail.

For I could tell you a story which is true;
I know a lady with a terrible tongue,
15 Blear ° eyes fallen from blue,
All her perfections tarnished—yet it is not long
Since she was lovelier than any of you.

John Crowe Ransom (1888–1974)

A Question-Commentary for this poem will be found on pg. 108.

° *fillets:* ribbons
° *publish:* make widely known
° *Blear:* dim, washed out

Sigh No More, Ladies

Sigh no more, ladies, sigh no more
    Men were deceivers ever,
One foot in sea and one on shore,
    To one thing constant never.
5   Then sigh not so, but let them go,
    And be you blithe and bonny,
Converting all your sounds of woe
    Into Hey nonny, nonny.

Sing no more ditties, sing no moe
10   Of dumps ° so dull and heavy.
The fraud of men was ever so,
    Since summer first was leavy.
Then sigh not so, but let them go,
    And be you blithe and bonny,
15   Converting all your sounds of woe
    Into Hey nonny, nonny.

from *Much Ado about Nothing* II, iii
William Shakespeare (1564–1616)

A Question-Commentary for this poem will be found on pg. 109.

° *dumps :* gloomy thoughts

SOME SAINTS AND SINNERS

5^a

Miniver Cheevy

Miniver Cheevy, child of scorn,
    Grew lean while he assailed the seasons;
He wept that he was ever born,
    And he had reasons.

5   Miniver loved the days of old
        When swords were bright and steeds were
            prancing;
    The vision of a warrior bold
        Would set him dancing.

Miniver sighed for what was not,
10   And dreamed, and rested from his labors;
    He dreamed of Thebes and Camelot,
        And Priam's neighbors.

Miniver mourned the ripe renown
        That made so many a name so fragrant;
15   He mourned Romance, now on the town,
        And Art, a vagrant.

Miniver loved the Medici,
        Albeit he had never seen one;
He would have sinned incessantly
20   Could he have been one.

Miniver cursed the commonplace
        And eyed a khaki suit with loathing;
He missed the medieval grace
        Of iron clothing.

25   Miniver scorned the gold he sought,

But sore annoyed was he without it;
Miniver thought, and thought, and thought,
    And thought about it.

Miniver Cheevy, born too late,
30   Scratched his head and kept on thinking;
Miniver coughed, and called it fate,
    And kept on drinking.

                    Edwin Arlington Robinson (1869–1935)

A Question-Commentary for this poem will be found on pg. 109.

5^b

The Gift to Be Simple

Breathing something German at the end,
Which no one understood, he died, a friend,
    Or so he meant to be, to all of us.
    Only the stars defined his radius;
5   His life, restricted to a wooden house,
Was in his head. He saw a fledgling fall.
    Two times he tried to nest it, but it fell
    Once more, and died; he wandered home again—
We save so plain a story for great men.
10   An angel in ill-fitting sweaters,
            Writing children naive letters,
    A violin player lacking vanities,
    A giant wit among the homilies—
We have no parallel to that immense
15   Intelligence.

But if he were remembered for the Bomb,
As some may well remember him, such a tomb,
    For one who hated violence and ceremony
    Equally, would be a wasted irony.
20   He flew to formal heavens from his perch,
A scientist become his own research,
    And even if the flames were never gold
    That lapped his body to an ash gone cold,

Even if his death no trumpets tolled,
25   There is enough of myth inside the truth
        To make a monument to fit him with;
And since the universe is in a jar,
There is no weeping where his heavens are,
And I would remember, now the world is less,
30   His gentleness.

Howard Moss (1921–   )

A Question-Commentary for this poem will be found on pg. 109.

5ᶜ

A Satirical Elegy

His Grace! impossible! what dead!
Of old age too, and in his bed!
And could that Mighty Warrior fall?
And so inglorious, after all!
5 Well, since he's gone, no matter how,
The last loud trump must wake him now:
And trust me, as the noise grows stronger,
He'd wish to sleep a little longer.
And could he be indeed so old
10 As by the news-papers we're told?
Threescore, I think, is pretty high;
'Twas time in conscience he should die.
This world he cumber'd ° long enough;
He burnt his candle to the snuff; °
15 And that's the reason, some folks think,
He left behind *so great a s—k.*
Behold his funeral appears,
Nor widow's sighs, nor orhpan's tears,
Wont ° at such times each heart to pierce,
20 Attend the progress of his herse.
But what of that, his friends may say,
He had those honours in his day.

° *cumber'd:* cluttered up
° *snuff:* the charred part of a candlewick
° *Wont:* accustomed

True to his profit and his pride,
He made them weep before he dy'd.
25   Come hither, all ye empty things,
Ye bubbles rais'd by breath of Kings;
Who float upon the tide of state,
Come hither, and behold your fate.
Let pride be taught by this rebuke,
30   How very mean a thing's a Duke;
From all his ill-got honours flung,
Turn'd to that dirt from whence he sprung.

Jonathan Swift (1667–1745)

A Question-Commentary for this poem will be found on pg. 109.

5^d

He Was

a brown old man with a green thumb:
I can remember the screak on stones of his hoe,
The chug, choke, and high madrigal wheeze
Of the spray-cart bumping below
5   The sputtery leaves of the apple trees,
But he was all but dumb

Who filled some quarter of the day with sound
All of my childhood long. For all I heard
Of all his labors, I can now recall
10   Never a single word
Until he went in the dead of fall
To the drowsy underground,

Having planted a young orchard with so great care
In that last year that none was lost, and May
15   Aroused them all, the leaves saying the land's
Praise for the livening clay,
And the found voice of his buried hands
Rose in the sparrowy air.

Richard Wilbur (1921–   )

A Question-Commentary for this poem will be found on pg. 110.

5ᵉ

My Last Duchess

That's my last Duchess painted on the wall,
Looking as if she were alive. I call
That piece a wonder, now: Frà Pandolf's ° hands
Worked busily a day, and there she stands.
5   Will 't please you sit and look at her? I said
"Frà Pandolf" by design, for never read
Strangers like you that pictured countenance,
The depth and passion of its earnest glance,
But to myself they turned (since none puts by
10   The curtain I have drawn for you, but I)
And seemed as they would ask me, if they durst,°
How such a glance came there; so, not the first
Are you to turn and ask thus. Sir, 'twas not
Her husband's presence only, called that spot
15   Of joy into the Duchess' cheek: perhaps
Frà Pandolf chanced to say, "Her ° mantle laps
Over my lady's wrist too much," or "Paint
Must never hope to reproduce the faint
Half-flush that dies along her throat:" such stuff
20   Was courtesy, she thought, and caused enough
For calling up that spot of joy. She had
A heart—how shall I say?—too soon made glad,
Too easily impressed; she liked whate'er
She looked on, and her looks went everywhere.
25   Sir, 'twas all one! My favor ° at her breast,
The dropping of the daylight in the West,
The bough of cherries some officious fool
Broke in the orchard for her, the white mule
She rode with round the terrace—all and each
30   Would draw from her alike the approving speech,
Or blush, at least. She thanked men,—good!
    but thanked
Somehow—I know not how—as if she ranked
My gift of a nine-hundred-years-old name
With anybody's gift. Who'd stoop to blame

° *Frà Pandolf:* name of the (imaginary) Renaissance artist who painted the
    portrait
° *durst:* dared
° *Her:* the artist uses the third person form as a mark of deference to nobility
° *favor:* i.e., gift

35 This sort of trifling? Even had you skill
    In speech—(which I have not)—to make your will
    Quite clear to such an one, and say, "Just this
    Or that in you disgusts me; here you miss,
    Or there exceed the mark"—and if she let
40 Herself be lessoned so, nor plainly set
    Her wits to yours, forsooth, and made excuse,
    —E'en then would be some stooping; and I choose
    Never to stoop. Oh sir, she smiled, no doubt,
    Whene'er I passed her; but who passed without
45 Much the same smile? This grew; I gave commands;
    Then all smiles stopped together. There she stands
    As if alive. Will 't please you rise? We'll meet
    The company below, then. I repeat,
    The Count your master's known munificence
50 Is ample warrant that no just pretense
    Of mine for dowry will be disallowed;
    Though his fair daughter's self, as I avowed
    At starting, is my object. Nay, we'll go
    Together down, sir. Notice Neptune,° though,
55 Taming a sea-horse, thought a rarity,
    Which Claus of Innsbruck ° cast in bronze for me!

                              Robert Browning (1812–1889)

A Question-Commentary for this poem will be found on pg. 110.

5ᶠ

Unwanted

The poster with my picture on it
Is hanging on the bulletin board in the Post Office.

I stand by it hoping to be recognized
Posing first full face and then profile

5   But everybody passes by and I have to admit
    The photograph was taken some years ago.

° *Neptune:* the sea-god
° *Claus of Innsbruck:* another imaginary Renaissance artist

I was unwanted then and I'm unwanted now
Ah guess ah'll go up echo mountain and crah.

I wish someone would find my fingerprints somewhere
10   Maybe on a corpse and say, You're it.

Description: Male, or reasonably so
White, but not lily-white and usually deep-red

Thirty-fivish, and looks it lately
Five-feet-nine and one-hundred-thirty pounds:
    no physique

15   Black hair going gray, hairline receding fast
What used to be curly, now fuzzy

Brown eyes starey under beetling brow
Mole on chin, probably will become a wen

It is perfectly obvious that he was not popular at school
20   No good at baseball, and wet his bed.

His aliases tell his history: Dumbell, Good-for-nothing,
Jewboy, Fieldinsky, Skinny, Fierce Face, Greaseball,
    Sissy.

Warning: This man is not dangerous, answers to
    any name
Responds to love, don't call him or he will come.

Edward Field (1924–   )

A Question-Commentary for this poem will be found on pg. 111.

5^g

Reason

Said, Pull her up a bit will you, Mac, I want to unload
    there.
Said, Pull her up my rear end, first come first serve.

Said, Give her the gun, Bud, he needs a taste of his own
    bumper.
Then the usher came out and got into the act:

5   Said, Pull her up, pull her up a bit, we need this space,
        sir.
    Said, For God's sake, is this still a free country
        or what?
    You go back and take care of Gary Cooper's horse
    And leave me handle my own car.

    Saw them unloading the lame old lady,
10 Ducked out under the wheel and gave her an elbow,
    Said, All you needed to do was just explain;
    Reason, Reason is my middle name.

                            Josephine Miles (1911–   )

A Question-Commentary for this poem will be found on pg. 111.

SOME NATURAL WAYS
OF BEING

6ᵃ

The Snow

It sifts from leaden sieves,
It powders all the wood,
It fills with alabaster wool
The wrinkles of the road.

5   It makes an even face
Of mountain and of plain,—
Unbroken forehead from the east
Unto the east again.

It reaches to the fence,
10   It wraps it, rail by rail,
Till it is lost in fleeces;
It flings a crystal veil

On stump and stack and stem,—
The summer's empty room,
15   Acres of seams where harvests were,
Recordless, but for them.

It ruffles wrists of posts
As ankles of a queen,—
Then stills its artisans like ghosts,
20   Denying they have been.

Emily Dickinson (1830–1886)

A Question-Commentary for this poem will be found on pg. 112.

Winter Seascape

The sea runs back against itself
    With scarcely time for breaking wave
To cannonade a slatey shelf
    And thunder under in a cave

5   Before the next can fully burst.
    The headwind, blowing harder still,
Smooths it to what it was at first—
    A slowly rolling water-hill.

Against the breeze the breakers haste,
10   Against the tide their ridges run
And all the sea's a dappled waste
    Criss-crossing underneath the sun.

Far down the beach the ripples drag
    Blown backward, rearing from the shore,
15   And wailing gull and shrieking shag °
    Alone can pierce the ocean roar.

Unheard, a mongrel hound gives tongue,
    Unheard are shouts of little boys:
What chance has any inland lung
20   Against this multi-water noise?

Here where the cliffs alone prevail
    I stand exultant, neutral, free,
And from the cushion of the gale
    Behold a huge consoling sea.

John Betjeman (1916–   )

A Question-Commentary for this poem will be found on pg. 112.

° *shag:* large seabird

Mushrooms

Overnight, very
Whitely, discreetly,
Very quietly

Our toes, our noses
Take hold on the loam,
Acquire the air.

Nobody sees us,
Stops us, betrays us;
The small grains make room.

Soft fists insist on
Heaving the needles,
The leafy bedding,

Even the paving.
Our hammers, our rams,
Earless and eyeless,

Perfectly voiceless,
Widen the crannies,
Shoulder through holes. We

Diet on water,
On crumbs of shadow,
Bland-mannered, asking

Little or nothing.
So many of us!
So many of us!

We are shelves, we are
Tables, we are meek,
We are edible,

Nudgers and shovers
In spite of ourselves.
Our kind multiplies:

We shall by morning
Inherit the earth.
Our foot's in the door.

Sylvia Plath (1932–1963)

A Question-Commentary for this poem will be found on pg. 112.

6^d

New Hampshire, February

Nature had made them hide in crevices,
Two wasps so cold they looked like bark.
Why I do not know, but I took them
And I put them
5   In a metal pan, both day and dark.

Like God touching his finger to Adam
I felt, and thought of Michelangelo,
For whenever I breathed on them,
The slightest breath,
10   They leaped, and preened as if to go.

My breath controlled them always quite.
More sensitive than electric sparks
They came into life
Or they withdrew to ice,
15   While I watched, suspending remarks,

Then one in a blind career got out,
And fell to the kitchen floor. I
Crushed him with my cold ski boot,
By accident. The other
20   Had not the wit to try or die.

And so the other is still my pet.
The moral of this is plain.
But I will shirk it.
You will not like it. And
25   God does not live to explain.

Richard Eberhart (1904–   )

A Question-Commentary for this poem will be found on pg. 113.

The Cage

Take, then, this image for what it is worth:
the eagle that I saw once, loved where he stood,
a sad brown thing roosting like a hen on a pole.
He was, of course, a captive. It was the zoo.
5 The cage was round and domed and let in light
and some of the jigsawed blue of the sky.
(I was a boy then. Love was fiercely caged.)

Outside there were peacocks on the grass.
They strutted on the clipped lawn like
10 elegant ancestors, folding and unfolding
intricate fans adorned with magic eyes.
He was alone with scattered winks of sky
and broken weather. Bald as a monk,
he seldom moved from his perch, never flew,

15 though there was room enough. He waited.
Sometimes he would stir, open his huge wings.
Then, I thought, seeing the beak and the cruel talons,
and the shadows of his wings like twin sails,
that nothing made of iron could keep him.
20 But that was only a whim, a ghostly gesture.
He wouldn't eat and so he died.

Afterwards there were still the peacocks to look at,
and all the small birds in their delicate cages,
and the rare ones with beaks and coloring to prove
25 God has a sense of humor in some climates.
But chiefly there was the cage like a great wound.
Like an eye put out, like space where a tree has been.
Wind howled in that empty place and I wanted to pray.

George Garrett (1929–   )

A Question-Commentary for this poem will be found on pg. 113.

6^f

Pied ° Beauty

Glory be to God for dappled things—
    For skies of couple-colour as a brinded ° cow;
        For rose-moles all in stipple ° upon trout that
        swim;
Fresh-firecoal chestnut-falls; finches' wings;
5   Landscape plotted and pieced—fold, fallow, and
        plough;
      And áll trádes, their gear and tackle and trim.
All things counter,° original, spare,° strange;
    Whatever is fickle, freckled (who knows how?)
      With swift, slow; sweet, sour; adazzle, dim;
10 He fathers-forth whose beauty is past change:
          Praise him.

Gerard Manley Hopkins (1844–1889)

A Question-Commentary for this poem will be found on pg. 113.

6^g

The Tom-cat

At midnight in the alley
    A Tom-cat comes to wail,
And he chants the hate of a million years
    As he swings his snaky tail.

5 Malevolent, bony, brindled,
    Tiger and devil and bard,
His eyes are coals from the middle of Hell
    And his heart is black and hard.

He twists and crouches and capers

° *Pied:* having two or more colors in patches
° *brinded:* brindled (having dark streaks on a fawn-colored background)
° *stipple:* colored dots
° *counter:* opposite
° *spare:* rare

10   And bares his curved sharp claws,
And he sings to the stars of the jungle nights
        Ere cities were, or laws.

Beast from a world primeval,
        He and his leaping clan,
15 When the blotched red moon leers over the roofs
        Give voice to their scorn of man.

He will lie on a rug tomorrow
        And lick his silky fur,
And veil the brute in his yellow eyes
20   And play he's tame, and purr.

But at midnight in the alley
        He will crouch again and wail,
And beat the time for his demon's song
        With the swing of his demon's tail.

                              Don Marquis (1878–1937)

A Question-Commentary for this poem will be found on pg. 114.

A Question-Commentary for this poem will be found on pg. 114.

Poems for Performing

SOME ODDITIES AND ENDS
(AND NO QUESTIONS ASKED)

7ᵃ

An Elegy on the Death of a Mad Dog

Good people all, of every sort,
    Give ear unto my song;
And if you find it wondrous short,
    It cannot hold you long.

5   In Islington there was a man
    Of whom the world might say,
That still a godly race he ran,
    Whene'er he went to pray.

A kind and gentle heart he had,
10   To comfort friends and foes:
The naked every day he clad,
    When he put on his clothes.

And in that town a dog was found,
    As many dogs there be,
15   Both mongrel, puppy, whelp, and hound,
    And curs of low degree.

This dog and man at first were friends;
    But when a pique began,
The dog, to gain some private ends,
20   Went mad, and bit the man.

Around from all the neighboring streets
    The wondering neighbors ran,
And swore the dog had lost his wits,
    To bite so good a man.

25   The wound it seemed both sore and sad
    To every Christian eye:

And while they swore the dog was mad,
    They swore the man would die.

But soon a wonder came to light
30   That showed the rogues they lied:
The man recovered of the bite,
    The dog it was that died.

Oliver Goldsmith (1730–1774)

7^b

The Latest Decalogue °

Thou shalt have one God only; who
Would be at the expense of two?
No graven images may be
Worshiped, except the currency.
5 Swear not at all; for, for thy curse
Thine enemy is none the worse.
At church on Sunday to attend
Will serve to keep the world thy friend.
Honor thy parents; that is, all
10 From whom advancement may befall.
Thou shalt not kill; but need'st not strive
Officiously to keep alive.
Do not adultery commit;
Advantage rarely comes of it.
15 Thou shalt not steal; an empty feat,
When it's so lucrative to cheat.
Bear not false witness; let the lie
Have time on its own wings to fly.
Thou shalt not covet, but tradition
20 Approves all forms of competition.

The sum of all is, thou shalt love,
If any body, God above:
At any rate shall never labor
More than thyself to love thy neighbor.

Arthur Hugh Clough (1819–1861)

° *Decalogue:* Ten Commandments

Father William

"You are old, Father William," the young man said,
    "And your hair has become very white;
And yet you incessantly stand on your head—
    Do you think, at your age, it is right?"

5   "In my youth," Father William replied to his son,
    "I feared it might injure the brain;
But now that I'm perfectly sure I have none,
    Why, I do it again and again."

"You are old," said the youth, "as I mentioned before,
10   And have grown most uncommonly fat;
Yet you turned a back somersault in at the door—
    Pray, what is the reason of that?"

"In my youth," said the sage, as he shook his gray locks,
    "I kept all my limbs very supple
15   By the use of this ointment—one shilling the box—
    Allow me to sell you a couple."

"You are old," said the youth, "and your jaws are too
    weak
    For anything tougher than suet;
Yet you finished the goose, with the bones and the beak;
20   Pray, how did you manage to do it?"

"In my youth," said his father, "I took to the law,
    And argued each case with my wife;
And the muscular strength which it gave to my jaw,
    Has lasted the rest of my life."

25   "You are old," said the youth; "one would hardly
    suppose
    That your eye was as steady as ever;
Yet you balanced an eel on the end of your nose—
    What made you so awfully clever?"

"I've answered three questions, and that is enough,"
30   Said his father; "don't give yourself airs!
Do you think I can listen all day to such stuff?
      Be off, or I'll kick you down-stairs!"

Lewis Carroll (1832–1898)

7ᵈ

Unwelcome

When we were young, we were merry, we were very very
      wise,
      And the door stood open at our feast,
When there passed us a woman with the West in her
      eyes,
      And a man with his back to the East.

5   O, still grew the hearts that were beating so fast,
      The loudest voice was still.
The jest died away on our lips as they passed,
      And the rays of July struck chill.

The cups of red wine turned pale on the board,
10   The white bread black as soot.
The hound forgot the hand of her lord,
      She fell down at his foot.

Low let me lie, where the dead dog lies,
      Ere I sit me down again at a feast,
15   When there passes a woman with the West in her eyes,
      And a man with his back to the East.

Mary Coleridge (1861–1907)

The Deacon's Masterpiece
Or, The Wonderful "One-Hoss Shay" °

Have you heard of the wonderful one-hoss shay,
That was built in such a logical way
It ran a hundred years to a day,
And then, of a sudden, it—ah, but stay,
5   I'll tell you what happened without delay,
Scaring the parson into fits,
Frightening people out of their wits,—
Have you ever heard of that, I say?

Seventeen hundred and fifty-five,
10   *Georgius Secundus* ° was then alive,—
Snuffy old drone from the German hive;
That was the year when Lisbon-town
Saw the earth open and gulp her down,
And Braddock's army was done so brown,
15   Left without a scalp to its crown.
It was on the terrible Earthquake-day
That the Deacon finished the one-hoss shay.

Now in building of chaises, I tell you what,
There is always *somewhere* a weakest spot,—
20   In hub, tire, felloe,° in spring or thill,°
In panel, or crossbar, or floor, or sill,
In screw, bolt, thoroughbrace,—lurking still,
Find it somewhere you must and will,—
Above or below, within or without,—
25   And that's the reason, beyond a doubt,
That a chaise *breaks down*, but doesn't *wear out*.

But the Deacon swore, (as Deacons do,
With an "I dew vum," or an "I tell *yeou*,")
He would build one shay to beat the taown
30   'N' the keounty 'n' all the kentry raoun';

° *Shay:* the French word "chaise" (see line 26), meaning "carriage," is pro-
nounced "shays," mistaken by some speakers as plural; by them "shay" is
considered the singular form
° *Georgius Secundus:* George II, King of England at the time
° *felloe:* rim of wheel
° *thill:* shaft

It should be so built that it couldn't break daown;
"Fur," said the Deacon, " 't's mighty plain
That the weakes' place mus' stan' the strain;
'N' the way t' fix it, uz I maintain, is only jest
T' make that place uz strong uz the rest."

So the Deacon inquired of the village folk
Where he could find the strongest oak,
That couldn't be split nor bent nor broke,—
That was for spokes and floor and sills;
He sent for lancewood to make the thills;
The crossbars were ash, from the straightest trees,
The panels of white-wood, that cuts like cheese,
But lasts like iron for things like these;
The hubs of logs from the "Settler's ellum,"—
Last of its timber,—they couldn't sell 'em,
Never an axe had seen their chips,
And the wedges flew from between their lips,
Their blunt ends frizzled like celery-tips;
Step and prop-iron, bolt and screw,
Spring, tire, axle, and linchpin too,
Steel of the finest, bright and blue;
Thoroughbrace bison-skin, thick and wide;
Boot, top, dasher, from tough old hide
Found in the pit when the tanner died.
That was the way he "put her through."—
"There!" said the Deacon, "naow she'll dew!"

Do! I tell you, I rather guess
She was a wonder, and nothing less!
Colts grew horses, beards turned gray,
Deacon and deaconess dropped away,
Children and grandchildren—where were they?
But there stood the stout old one-hoss shay
As fresh as on Lisbon-earthquake-day!

EIGHTEEN HUNDRED; it came and found
The Deacon's masterpiece strong and sound.
Eighteen hundred increased by ten;—
"Hahnsum kerridge" they called it then.
Eighteen hundred and twenty came;—
Running as usual; much the same.
Thirty and forty at last arrive,
And then came fifty, and FIFTY-FIVE.

Little of all we value here
Wakes on the morn of its hundredth year
Without both feeling and looking queer.
75   In fact, there's nothing that keeps its youth,
So far as I know, but a tree and truth.
(This is a moral that runs at large;
Take it.—You're welcome.—No extra charge.)

FIRST OF NOVEMBER,—The Earthquake-day
80   There are traces of age in the one-hoss shay,
A general flavor of mild decay,
But nothing local, as one may say.
There couldn't be,—for the Deacon's art
Had made it so like in every part
85   That there wasn't a chance for one to start.
For the wheels were just as strong as the thills,
And the floor was just as strong as the sills,
And the panels just as strong as the floor,
And the whipple-tree neither less nor more,
90   And the back-crossbar as strong as the fore,
And spring and axle and hub *encore.*
And yet, *as a whole*, it is past a doubt,
In another hour it will be *worn out!*

First of November, 'Fifty-five!
95   This morning the parson takes a drive.
Now, small boys, get out of the way!
Here comes the wonderful one-hoss shay,
Drawn by a rat-tailed, ewe-necked bay.
"Huddup!" said the parson.—Off went they.

100   The parson was working his Sunday's text,—
Had got to *fifthly,* and stopped perplexed
And what the—Moses—was coming next.
All at once the horse stood still,
Close by the meet'n'-house on the hill.
105   —First a shiver, and then a thrill,
Then something decidedly like a spill,—
And the parson was sitting upon a rock,
At half past nine by the meet'n'-house clock,—
Just the hour of the Earthquake shock!
110   —What do you think the parson found.

When he got up and stared around?
The poor old chaise in a heap or mound,
As if it had been to the mill and ground!
You see, of course, if you're not a dunce,
115 How it went to pieces all at once,—
All at once, and nothing first,—
Just as bubbles do when they burst.

End of the wonderful one-hoss shay
Logic is logic. That's all I say.

Oliver Wendell Holmes (1809–1894)

7 f

Mr. Artesian's Conscientiousness

Once there was a man named Mr. Artesian and his
      activity was tremendous,
And he grudged every minute away from his desk be-
      cause the importance of his work was so stupendous;
5 And he had one object all sublime,
Which was to save simply oodles of time.
He figured that sleeping eight hours a night meant that
      if he lived to be seventy-five he would have spent
      twenty-five years not at his desk but in bed,
10 So he cut his slumber to six hours which meant he only
      lost eighteen years and nine months instead,
And he figured that taking ten minutes for breakfast
      and twenty minutes for luncheon and half an hour
      for dinner meant that he spent three years, two
15 months and fifteen days at the table,
So that by subsisting solely on bouillon cubes which he
      swallowed at his desk to save this entire period he
      was able,
And he figured that at ten minutes a day he spent a little
20 over six months and ten days shaving,
So he grew a beard, which gave him a considerable saving,
And you might think that now he might have been

satisfied, but no, he wore a thoughtful frown,

Because he figured that at two minutes a day he would
25   spend thirty-eight days and a few minutes in
elevators just traveling up and down,

So as a final timesaving device he stepped out the
window of his office, which happened to be on the
fiftieth floor,

30   And one of his partners asked "Has he vertigo?" and
the other glanced out and down and said "Oh no,
only about ten feet more."

Ogden Nash (1902–1971)

7ᵍ

The Jumblies

I

They went to sea in a Sieve, they did,
   In a Sieve they went to sea:
In spite of all their friends could say,
On a winter's morn, on a stormy day,
5   In a Sieve they went to sea!
And when the Sieve turned round and round,
And every one cried, 'You'll all be drowned!'
They called aloud, 'Our Sieve ain't big,
But we don't care a button! we don't care a fig!
10   In a Sieve we'll go to sea!"
      Far and few, far and few,
        Are the lands where the Jumblies live;
        Their heads are green, and their hands are blue,
        And they went to sea in a Sieve.

II

15   They sailed away in a Sieve, they did,
   In a Sieve they sailed so fast,
With only a beautiful pea-green veil
Tied with a riband by way of a sail,
   To a small tobacco-pipe mast;
20   And every one said, who saw them go,
'O won't they be soon upset, you know!

For the sky is dark, and the voyage is long,
And happen what may, it's extremely wrong
   In a Sieve to sail so fast!'
25   Far and few, far and few,
       Are the lands where the Jumblies live;
     Their heads are green, and their hands are blue,
     And they went to sea in a Sieve.

III

The water it soon came in, it did,
30   The water it soon came in;
So to keep them dry, they wrapped their feet
In a pinky paper all folded neat,
   And they fastened it down with a pin.
And they passed the night in a crockery-jar,
35 And each of them said, 'How wise we are!
Though the sky be dark, and the voyage be long,
Yet we never can think we were rash or wrong,
   While round in our Sieve we spin!'
     Far and few, far and few,
40   Are the lands where the Jumblies live;
     Their heads are green, and their hands are blue,
     And they went to sea in a Sieve.

IV

And all night long they sailed away;
   And when the sun went down,
45 They whistled and warbled a moony song
To the echoing sound of a coppery gong,
   In the shade of the mountains brown.
'O Timballoo! How happy we are,
When we live in a Sieve and a crockery-jar,
50 And all night long in the moonlight pale,
We sail away with a pea-green sail,
   In the shade of the mountains brown!'
     Far and few, far and few,
       Are the lands where the Jumblies live;
55   Their heads are green, and their hands are blue,
     And they went to sea in a Sieve.

V

They sailed to the Western Sea, they did,
   To a land all covered with trees,

And they bought an Owl, and a useful Cart,
60 And a pound of Rice, and a Cranberry Tart,
    And a hive of silvery Bees.
And they bought a Pig, and some green Jack-daws,
And a lovely Monkey with lollipop paws,
And forty bottles of Ring-Bo-Ree,
65   And no end of Stilton Cheese.
     Far and few, far and few,
      Are the lands where the Jumblies live;
    Their heads are green, and their hands are blue,
    And they went to sea in a Sieve.

VI

70 And in twenty years they all came back,
    In twenty years or more,
And every one said, 'How tall they've grown!
For they've been to the Lakes, and the Torrible Zone,
    And the hills of the Chankly Bore';
75 And they drank their health, and gave them a feast
Of dumplings made of beautiful yeast;
And every one said, 'If we only live,
We too will go to sea in a Sieve,—
    To the hills of the Chankly Bore!'
80   Far and few, far and few,
      Are the lands where the Jumblies live;
    Their heads are green, and their hands are blue,
    And they went to sea in a Sieve.

Edward Lear (1812–1888)

PART III

Ways In

*Question-Commentaries
on Poems in Parts I and II*

The following question-commentaries on each poem in Parts I and II are meant to be used in the way the title of this part suggests—as "ways in" to the poems they are paired with. It may well be that a given poem seems to offer no problems, but then again it may offer problems that you don't see. As we said in the Introduction, these "ways in" are suggestive only, and they shouldn't be looked on as testing devices or puzzles with a discoverable solution.

For an example of the kinds of questions that can be asked (the kinds that a reader has to eventually ask for himself) and the possible ways they can be responded to, read the following poem by Robert Frost and then our responses to some questions that might profitably be asked about it:

The Door in the Dark

In going from room to room in the dark
I reached out blindly to save my face,
But neglected, however lightly, to lace
My fingers and close my arms in an arc.
A slim door got in past my guard,
And hit me a blow in the head so hard
I had my native simile jarred.
So people and things don't pair any more
With what they used to pair with before.

One kind of "question" might simply deal with getting the picture straight. Most poems mean what they say, even though they mean, in a sense, more than they say. Sometimes the delight of the verbal play and rhythm lulls us into ignoring the obvious, common-sense statements being made. An opening question on "The Door in the Dark" might go:

Describe the speaker's actions as he moves from "room to room in the dark." He mentions having a "guard." What was he doing to protect himself? What does he realize he should have been doing?

The poet is clearly expecting the reader to bring up from memory into imaginative focus an experience everyone has had—going from room to room in the pitch-dark. You remember the groping, even fearful way you budge along, expecting every moment to rap a shin, stub a toe, black an eye. You swing your arms in cautious circles, maybe even "lace [your] fingers," feeling for solid surfaces. Frost describes this simple experience, detailing the precautions taken to protect one's most vulnerable part—the face.

The reader with his eyes open is also going to notice details of the language used in the opening description and ask himself what further suggestions about the poem's meaning they might offer: such phrases as "save my face" in line 2 and "past my guard" in line 5. They help in defining the actions during the "blind" groping, but they might also define an attitude in the mind of the "blind" groper: with what activity is a phrase like "past my guard" usually associated? and what is "save my face" (or "saving face") usually associated with?

Another kind of "question" related to getting the picture straight might focus on unusual words or phrases, unusual in the sense of being out of a normal context or suggesting a different from normal point of view. For instance:

> What kind of door is a "slim door"? Why does the speaker say that the door "hit [him] a blow in the head" rather than saying, as would be normal and logical, that he walked into it?

A "slim door" is one that is open so that one looks at it or, in this case, encounters it from the thin side. ("Slim" also suggests, ironically, that there's not much to it.) No matter if a person admits to himself that he "neglected" (line 3) to use the proper precaution, the fact of running head-on into the thin edge of an open door makes him react to the lifeless door as if it were alive and capable of delivering a blow. (Have you ever kicked a chair after stubbing your toe against it?) When one does something careless or stupid, he automatically looks for someone or something else to blame.

Another question on how language is working in the poem might be:

> What is a "simile"? What does the phrase "native simile" mean? (What meaning of "native" applies best here? Or do several of its meanings apply equally well? Don't be afraid to look at the dictionary.)

A simile is what English teachers call a "figure of speech." Specifically, it's a use of language that explicitly links one thing with certain qualities of another thing: "legs like splints (or stumps)," "a pitching arm like a flail," "soft as rain," "My love is like a red, red rose." (Langston Hughes's poem, *Harlem*, is built as a series of similes that begins: "What happens to a dream deferred? / Does it dry up / like a raisin in the sun?")

Since "native" can mean "natural," "normal," "simple," "inborn," "unaffected," among other things, the idea behind "native simile" is the ability to make the obvious, uncomplicated, unstartling connections when pairing (= seeing samenesses and differences) people and things, which is the kind of pairing most of us make in our ordinary, everyday, uncomplicated, sensible existences.

Another kind of "question" might bring up suggestions of "larger meanings," observations on human behavior in general. There are many ways in which these suggestions might be raised. One way might be to ask what would be lost if the poem were different from what it actually is, and in that way get at what the "actually is" is:

> If the poem ended with line seven changed to, "I had my simple senses jarred," what meanings that the poem now has would be lost? Why?

With this shortened version (with no mention of the "native simile" being "jarred"), the speaker is still not just talking about an unfortunate meeting with a door in the dark. The door is still treated as an active agent in the encounter, not just an innocent bystander, and the speaker still recognizes that his neglect to "lace [his] fingers" brought about the smack in the head. Is he saying that the world *out there*—"alive" in the normal sense of the word or not— is just waiting for people to drop their "guard," to be negligent, so that a senses-jarring reminder of the consequences of carelessness or neglect, "however light," can be promptly delivered? In other words, does the hit in the head *stand for* all those experiences in which one gets his comeuppance for being neglectful?

But the poem doesn't end the way the shortened version does, and while the generalized comment on neglectfulness may still be suggested in Frost's original, it doesn't take into account that the speaker is saying something different from simply that he was knocked silly by a door (people get over that). What the last three lines say is that something specific in the speaker was knocked out of kilter and that the blow had lasting consequences.

The specific thing is connected somehow with similes: uses of language where two largely unlike things are seen as having certain likenesses, as we have said. And it is the speaker's "native simile," the kind his upbringing and normal behavior would suggest to him, that is changed forever. So, the "blow in the head" knocked his language-using power out of whack, a convenient and slightly whacky explanation of why he is a poet, since what a poet does is to take a nonnormal look at the so-called normal world; he pairs "people and things . . . with what they [didn't] used to pair with before"; he de-expectancies the expected; he throws you a curve when you're looking for the fast ball; he gets a stiff left jab "past [your] guard."

Beyond that, perhaps, for sensitive (and alert) readers, an experience such as Frost describes can forever upset our useful stock pairings, our commonplace "wisdoms" or orthodoxies: our unrecognized or unadmitted racism, for instance, or our self-serving jingoism, or our cultural smugness.

Part I   Question-Commentaries

1.   The Young Ones, Flip Side

1. Why does the writer call his poem the "flip side" of "the young ones"? What possible meanings are there of "flip"? Which ones fit best here? Why?
2. In line 8 what is appropriate about the word "usurping" as applied to "rouge". Upon what does the rouge usurp? How can "stance," "rouge," "glance," and "hips" all *hide* youth's doubt? What sort of doubt is this?
3. Is there more than one meaning in "Put off" and "put on"? By "It's gone" does the speaker mean the same thing as by "Put off"? Explain.
4. How old is the speaker? How do you know? Why does he (she) think that "youth hurts"? In what sense does it hurt, according to the poem?
5. In your own opinion *does* "youth hurt"? Why or why not? Are there equivalent hurts in the other ages of life? If so, name some.

2.   I'm Nobody. Who Are You?

1. What has to be the answer to the question in the second line? Why? Read the first two lines aloud several times. Is there any

way you can read them so as to suggest that the response might be "no"?

2. Who are the "they" of line 4? How do you know? Why would "they" banish "nobodies"?

3. In what sense is a frog "public"? How can it be said that he "tells his name"? What's a bog to a frog? What else is a bog in this poem?

4. Would anything be lost if "the livelong June" were changed to read "the whole of June"? If so, what?

5. Why would anybody rather be a "nobody" than a "somebody"? Would you (even if your answer to line 2 was yes)? Does the speaker *really* think she's (he's) nobody? If you know that you're nobody, and if you prefer things that way, are you really nobody?

3.   Dust of Snow

1. What would be factually wrong about changing "hemlock tree" in line 4 to "great oak tree"? What would be factually wrong if the first word of line 2 were "Dumped" instead of "Shook"?

2. Did the crow shake the snow on the speaker on purpose? Does the speaker think it did? How do you know? Does it make any difference? What possible difference would the "way" (line 1) the crow supposedly did it have?

3. How does the speaker feel about being dusted with snow by a crow? How did he feel before he got dusted? How did he feel after? How do you know?

4.   Résumé

1. What is a résumé? Why is the title appropriate?

2. Why is the poem funny? Why would it be less funny if the last line read: "Wake up and live!"? Why would it be less funny if line 5 read: "Guns hurt awful"?

3. What does the clipped sentence structure—eight short and complete statements—contribute to the effect of the poem? Would it be more or less effective if it read as follows:

> They say that razors pain you,
> And that rivers are cold and wet,
> And that acids sort of stain you,
> And drugs bring cramps and sweat;

They say that guns aren't lawful,
And that nooses have been known to give,
And that gas smells something awful,
So why not give up and live.

Why?

5.   The Clod and the Pebble

1. Contrast the two views of love expressed by the clod and the pebble.
2. Why is a "clod of clay" the appropriate speaker for stanza 1 and a "pebble of the brook" the appropriate speaker for stanza 3?

6.   The Amish

1. Why does the speaker call the Amish a "surly sect"? Who thinks so?
2. How can it be argued that "regrets" fits in perfectly with the rest of the items listed in stanza 2?
3. What's a synonym for "undivine"? Why is "undivine" a much more telling word than any synonym for it would be?
4. "Licensed fools" in former times (often kept by kings and often referred to as "court jesters") were so-called because they were given "license," i.e. permission, to speak derisively and insultingly. The moderns who drive to Amish country are "licensed fools" in this sense, says the poem—but in what other sense also (consider the pun in "licensed")?
5. We normally talk of "revoking a license," but in stanza 4 the speaker wants Jehovah (why not "God"?) to "revoke the licensed fools" who travel to Amish country to "gaze." What is gained by the switch? How can people be "revoked"?
6. What kind of person is the speaker? Does he like the Amish? How do you know? Do you, based on what he says? Why or why not?

7.   Esthete in Harlem

1. What is the effect of the speaker's calling Harlem "this nigger place"? What meanings do you think the word carries for him?

What are some of the things he may mean by calling the street "vile"?

2. In what ways exactly do you see "Life" in Harlem "stepping on" the speaker's feet? Does he like the experience? Dislike it? How do you know? Why is "Life" in line 7 capitalized?

3. What is the meaning and effect of the one word, "Strange," standing alone as the first line? What would be lost if the poem began:

> It's strange that in this nigger place
> I should meet life face to face—

4. What is an "esthete"? Why does the speaker call himself one? Can the two nouns of the title be regarded as in some sense opposites? Why or why not?

8.   A Choice of Weapons

1. What kind of person is the speaker? How old is he/she? How do you know? (Who would say "Words can sting like anything"?) Does what the poem says apply just to people like the speaker or to everybody?

2. The poem obviously depends for part of its meaning on the old nursery rhyme:

> Sticks and stones can break my bones,
> But names can never hurt me.

How true is that sentiment? How is the poem's sentiment different from the nursery rhyme's? How true is the poem's sentiment?

3. Give an example from everyday experience of the way in which silence might break a heart.

4. What does the title have reference to? Why is it appropriate here?

9.   Which Is My Little Boy

1. You don't have to speak French to learn how to pronounce the lines with French in them. Have someone who speaks French well read them aloud, and then use that pronunciation as a guide. Once you've repeated the poem several times, the French will be easy to pronounce acceptably (it fits the English very well).

2. Grade the following statements A, B, C, D according as they seem

to you more or less true in the light of the evidence supplied by
the poem:

a. *Jean qui rit* is sick.
b. *Jean qui pleure* is going to die.
c. *Jean qui rit* is younger than *Jean qui pleure*.
d. *Jean qui rit* reminds the speaker of his childhood.
e. *Jean qui pleure* reminds the speaker of his approaching old age.
f. *Jean qui pleure* reminds the speaker of childhood's grave moods.
g. *Jean qui rit* reminds the speaker of childhood's gay moods.
h. *Jean qui pleure* reminds the speaker that in a child (as in an
   acorn) grandeurs lurk.
i. *Jean qui pleure* and *Jean qui rit* represent two primary aspects
   of human experience.
j. *Jean qui rit* and *Jean qui pleure* are both the same little boy.
k. There is an answer to the question asked in lines 1–2 and 11–12.

10.   The End of the World

1. Describe specifically what's going on in the first eight lines. What
   is gained by keeping suspended the promise of the opening words,
   "Quite unexpectedly. . . ."? How do the goings-on in lines 1–8
   support the idea that the event *is* quite unexpected? What
   might be going on instead if the event *had* been expected?
2. How does the movement of the last six lines differ from that of
   the first eight? What is the effect of the repetition of "there" in
   lines 9–13 and "nothing" in line 14?
3. How do the many proper names in lines 1–8 enhance the contrast
   between those lines and the last six? What would happen to the
   feeling created by the last six if they too were studded with
   familiar proper names?
4. What is gained by describing the end of the world in terms of
   the top blowing off a circus tent? In what respects might the
   "world" be regarded as a circus?

11.   The Sloth

1. What makes the sloth "Ex-as-per-at-ing"? Is being "Ex-as-per-
   at-ing" more of an exasperation than being "Exasperating"?
   Why?
2. What makes the speaker sure that "you just *know* he knows he

knows"? Do you? Why? Does the sloth care if you know he knows
he knows?
3. Try reading the poem to convey the idea that the speaker really
   is exasperated with the sloth. Is it possible? Then read it con-
   veying the idea that he is charmed by the sloth—and more than
   a little envious. Easy?
4. How would you explain the poet's use of capital letters?

12.   The Garden of Love

1. Describe the Garden of Love as the speaker first knew it. Consider
   especially lines 4 and 8. Then describe it as he finds it to be now.
2. What does "Thou shalt not" recall and what does it stand for
   here? What does the Chapel represent? With whom does the
   speaker compare the Priests by using the phrase "walking their
   rounds?" Why do they bind with *briars?*
3. What rhyme pattern set in stanzas 1 and 2 is discontinued in
   stanza 3? Can you account for the poet's doing this? In the same
   light, account for the rhythm change in the last two lines.

13.   archy confesses

The speaker here, archy, is a cockroach who writes poems on a
typewriter by jumping from key to key. Given the nature of type-
writers, he can't make capital letters or certain punctuation marks,
but neither is necessary.

1. Explain what a "fish wife curse" is. What is "the laugh of the
   horse"?
2. Be sure you know what "jocosity," "aesthetic," and "adduced"
   mean. Why do you suppose archy uses such big words in a poem
   about being "low browed" and "coarse"?
3. What convinces you that archy knows bill shakespeare quite well
   (even if you don't)?

14.   Much Madness Is Divinest Sense

1. Can the same person be both sane and mad in the light of this
   poem? How? What kinds of human concerns do you suppose the
   speaker is talking about? Give one or two examples, from history

or from your own experience, of supposed "madness" which you personally would want to name "divinest sense."

2. Is "sense" a quality of what has come to be called "The Establishment," i.e. the "official" values, views, and slogans of any society in any age, and "madness" a quality of its critics? Why or why not?

3. What problem does the poem raise but leave unanswered in contrasting "the discerning eye" against "the majority"? Is the majority necessarily always wrong? Who is to decide when the discerning eye *is* discerning and not self-deceiving? With what word in line 1 does the author indicate that she recognizes this problem?

15. The Eagle

1. What details in the poem show that the bird is described as if it were human? What is gained by so doing? Besides the obvious references (hands, walls, etc.), consider whether the speaker is simply looking at the bird or looking at the world through the bird's consciousness.

2. In reading the poem aloud, pay attention to how the rhyme scheme and the line structure force you to read it slowly and deliberately. What is the relationship between that patterning and what is being said about the eagle?

16. Upon Julia's Clothes

1. What quality in the silk of Julia's clothes is the speaker concerned with in the first stanza? How does the word *liquefaction* sum up this quality?

2. What causes the "brave vibration" of line 5? What does "each way free" mean? What quality is the speaker concerned with in stanza 2? What word sums it up?

3. How is the sense of "flowing" produced in the rhythm? Note particularly how line 2 moves into line 3, and line 4 into line 5. What is the effect of the rush of "Then, then, methinks . . ." (2) and "Oh, how that glittering taketh me" (6)?

4. Why isn't the title "Julia" instead of "Upon Julia's Clothes"?

17. The Debt

1. How does the line structure match—or help create—the mood of

the speaker? Consider the line length, where the syllable stresses
come, and the lack of any "flow" from line to line. How would
the effect be different if the first stanza, for instance, went like
this:

> All this sums up the debt I pay
> For just one sweet and riotous day:
> Long years of vain regret and grief,
> And sorrow tinged not with relief.

2. In everyday psychological (or religious?) terms what is the
   "debt" and what is the "interest"?
3. What kind of person would feel that he had taken on such a debt?
4. What emphasis do you give the word "God" in line 9? Why? What
   does the word mean to you here?

18.　The Pennycandystore Beyond the El

1. What is the "unreality" that the speaker "fell in love with"?
   What connection does the reference to the items in the pennycandystore have with the falling leaves, the rain-drenched girl,
   and the cry "Too soon! too soon!"?
2. In general terms how old is the speaker? How do you know? Why
   does he remember the pennycandystore and the happenings he
   connects with it?
3. What connections do you see between the meaning of this poem
   and "The Young Ones, Flip Side" (page 6)?

19.　Eldorado

1. What does line 21 recall? Who or what is the "pilgrim shadow"?
   What answer does he give to the knight's question?
2. Where or what is Eldorado? How does one get there or it? Why
   would anyone want to go there, or spend a lifetime searching for
   it? (We don't have any fixed "answer" in mind.)

20.　Silver

1. "Shoon" is the old plural of "shoe" (akin to "ox-oxen"). Can
   you think of any reason the poet might have used it other than
   to get a rhyme with "moon"?

2. What two closely related consonant sounds, more than any others, tie the poem together? How many occurrences of these sounds do you find all told? (We're talking about *sounds*, not spelling.) What other consonant or vowel sounds get extensive use?
3. Why is everything silver-colored? Is moonlight silver in color? What is the effect of using the word "silver" ten times in fourteen lines? (Consider both the images it creates and the echoing sound in the lines it appears in.) Who in the poem sees the world as silver-colored?
4. The first two words in the poem are "Slowly, silently. . . ." Can the poem be read in any other way than "slowly, silently"? Try it. What happens?

21.   They Told Me You Had Been to Her

1. Someone once commented about this poem (perhaps it was the White Rabbit's psychiatrist) that, "If you don't pay any attention to what it says, the poem makes a lot of sense." In what sense does it "make a lot of sense"? Read it aloud seriously, as if you thought that it makes sense. Listen to what it sounds like when someone else reads it aloud. What kinds of reports or conversations does it sound like?

22.   Girl's Song

1. What is the answer to the girl's question in the last two lines: 1) that she saw in the *old* man her *young* man and so recognized the human fate to age and die; or 2) that she saw in her young man the old man he will someday be and so recognized the human fate? Does it matter which? Why or why not?
2. Why did she "sit and cry"? What happened to her song and "fancy"?

23.   We Real Cool

1. What is the purpose of ending every line but the last with "We"? Why not the last?
2. What does "cool" mean in this poem? How "cool," in fact, were the "we" who say they are "real cool"? How do you know? How cool are they now?

3. What do "lurk late," "Strike straight," "Sing sin," "Thin gin,"
   and "Jazz June" mean? (There may be a number of possibilities,
   so share your suggestions.)
4. Try reading this chorally, with seven students playing the "Seven
   at the Golden Shovel."

24. This Is Just to Say

1. What is lost if the title isn't read as an essential part of the poem?
   Do you think that the person who was "probably saving" the
   plums is present as the speaker explains what he has done, or
   is the speaker writing a note about it, perhaps to leave on the
   kitchen table? Support your decision.
2. When do you think it dawned on the speaker that somebody was
   "probably saving" the plums "for breakfast"—before or after he
   ate them? How do you know? Is he sorry that he ate them? Or
   is "sorry" not quite the right word? (Is what he says after "Forgive me" a "reason" for doing what he did, or what?)
3. Do you think that the person who was saving the plums was upset by the fact that they were eaten? Why or why not? Given
   the kind of explanation the speaker makes, how do you think you
   would have reacted to his eating your plums and then asking you
   to forgive him?
4. What personal pronoun dominates the first stanza? the second
   stanza? What relationship does *Forgive me* in the third stanza
   bring these two pronouns (and the persons they stand for) into?
   Could it be argued that the three stanzas are like three scenes
   composing a short play? What would be the theme of that play?

25. Not Waving But Drowning

1. Why is the "him" of the poem referred to as "the dead man" if
   "still he lay moaning"? In what sense has he always been treated
   as if he were dead? Note lines 9 and 11–12. What does "cold"
   mean in line 7? in line 9?
2. What are the literal and nonliteral meanings of "further out" and
   "far out" in the poem? Imagine, if you can, the terror that would
   come over you if you were flailing your arms in panic trying to
   stay afloat and people on the shore simply waved at you, thinking
   they were gaily returning your greeting.
3. What kind of people are the "they" of the poem (line 8)? Con-

sider especially such phrases as "Poor chap" and "loved lark-ing," the simplistic explanation in line 7 of what happened to the man, and the fact that they don't hear a thing he says. Why is line 7 so long and line 8 so short? How are they meant to be read?

4. Have you ever felt in such a way that the phrase "not waving but drowning" would accurately characterize how other people were misunderstanding you? When and why?

Part II   Question-Commentaries

1. SOME PLANNED
AND UNPLANNED ENDINGS

1a.   Chorus

1. There's no end punctuation in the poem, even at the end. Is there any place where a period would normally go except at the end? If this is just one long sentence, why do you suppose the poet chose to make it so? Why no period at the end?
2. What connection has the song "Old MacDonald" got with what the poem is about and the unending way it's constructed?
3. Explain the meaning of:

   a. "a bolt fell from the compound interest problem" (What did "money" have to do with it?)
   b. "a rod broke in the third chapter of the Civicsbook" (What did violation of good government have to do with it?)
   c. "went sidewise over tirescreech" (What do you take to be the subject of "went"?)
   d. "its multitudinous self incarnadine" (*Incarnadine* is a verb here, *sea* is its subject, *self* its object. When you read Shake-speare's *Macbeth* you will find that the hero, looking at his bloody hands after he has murdered a sleeping man with his dagger, despairs of ever being able to wash them clean; even the whole ocean, he feels, cannot wash away *this* blood; rather the blood will "the multitudinous seas incarnadine," i.e. stain the sea red. Does knowing this about the phrase add some-thing to its value here? What?)

4. The word "panorama" is used twice. What is a "panorama" and how appropriate is Ciardi's use of it where he uses it?
5. How would you respond to someone who argued that the poet here treats a terrible tragedy as if it is no more important or serious than a happy day's outing or a child's painting of a summer scene?

1b.   A Moment Please

1. How did you read the poem the first time through? Line for line? Italics first, roman type second—or the other way around? How did you read it after you realized what the arrangement was? What do you think is the best way to read it? Why?
2. Why is the poem divided the way it is? Does the speaker answer the questions he raises in the italicized lines? If so, what are the answers? How do you know?
3. What is a "homeless clan"? Why is the phrase particularly appropriate here? How does it blend with "dupe of space" and "toy of time"?
4. What various meanings does the title have?
5. Did the "two adolescent girls" plan their meeting and attack? How do you know? Does the speaker expect what he gets—does he know that it's coming? Discuss.

1c.   Song

1. What happened? Trade interpretations, supporting your deductions with references to specific suggestions in the poem.
2. Do you think the stranger will be back? Why or why not?

1d.   *Vale* from Carthage

1. What do the following mean:

   a. "Wears doom, like dungarees, and doesn't know"
   b. "No furlough fluttered from the sky"
   c. "they laid / Upon his road of fire their sudden shade"
   d. "Living those words at Rome"
   e. "What's left but this to say of any war?"

2. What kind of person do you think the speaker is? The opening

of the poem seems almost brutally matter-of-fact. Is it? *Vale* means "farewell." What's the farewell here? What has the Roman soldier (killed at Carthage centuries ago in Rome's wars on Carthage) got to do with that farewell?

3. How many kinds of endings does the poem deal with? Which are planned and which not planned?

1e. Meeting at Night

1. What is the story that is suggested here, rather than told? Does the person in the farmhouse expect the "meeting"? How do you know?
2. Does the speaker's concentrating on the details of the trip, and not on the details of the girl, show that he doesn't really care about her? Or does it instead tell how keenly he cares? Explain.
3. How do you know it's the man going to meet the woman and not the other way around?
4. How does the sound of lines 5–6 support what is being said in them? What similar effect is there in lines 9–10?
5. How does the absence of verbs in lines 1–4 and 7–12 (and of main verbs everywhere) help convey the emotion of the lovers? What is the effect of having five lines begin with "and"?

1f. Exploration over the Rim

1. What does "over the rim" mean? The rim of what? Why would anyone want to "explore" beyond the "river's turning" or around "this corner" where a "certain danger" is?
2. Why does the speaker say that the "new country" is "safe from," rather than deprived of, "our learning"?
3. What does the last line mean? What ways of "burning" seem to be implied? Do you agree with the speaker's attitude? Why or why not?

1g. Molly Means

1. What is the effect of repeating (with slight changes) the last two lines of each stanza? How conscious is the speaker at all times of the "presence" of Molly Means? Read the poem aloud, giving special attention to how you handle the two-line refrain.

2. Try writing an extra stanza that fits the spirit of the poem. Put it in anywhere you like.

2. SOME SWEET
AND SOUR LOVE NOTES

2a.   Launcelot with Bicycle

1. If you don't know who the one-and-only, original Launcelot (Sir) was and what Astolat was, look them up. You might also look up Tennyson's "The Lady of Shalott," on which this poem is partially based. How has the poet used the Launcelot story as the background for her own? Why bring in Launcelot and Astolat in the first place—why not title the poem "Young Man with Bicycle" (or maybe "Spike with Bike")?
2. How old is the "anonymous and shy" viewer? How do you know? Does age make any difference? (How old was the Maid of Astolat?) How old is the speaker? Is she (he?) laughing at the viewer? How do you know? Are you? What for?
3. The time is April (when "maples at their bloom / Shake . . . pollen down like stars"). Could the same longing happen in October? Explain.

2b.   Vain Gratuities

1. If "gratuities" are things freely given with nothing expected in return, what are the gratuities here? What does "vain" mean in conjunction with gratuities?
2. What do you take to be the significance of lines 7 and 8?
3. How do you know that the woman spoken of doesn't see her husband the way the "other women" see him? How does she see him? Why do you suppose the others don't see him her way? How do you see him? Why?

2c.   Green Grow the Rashes

1. What does the first line have to do with what the speaker of the poem is talking about? What season does it announce? What setting?

2. What do you think the repeated "O's" do for the tone of the poem? Read it without the "O's." What's the difference?
3. If you're one of the "lasses O," do you agree with the speaker's sentiments? If you're one of the other, do you agree? Why or why not in either case?

2d.   Barbara Allan

1. Why did Barbara Allan reject Sir John? What do you think he saw in her in the first place? What killed him? What will kill her?
2. Is this a sweet or sour love note? Support your decision. What does your answer tell you about yourself?

2e.   For Hettie

1. What kind of person is the speaker? Do you suppose that he's a "good husband"? Why or why not? What does he expect from his wife? What does he get? How bothered is he that she is "left-handed" (in his eyes) in everything she does?
2. What does it show about him that he puts "black stockings" and "refusing to take orders" in the same breath? How are we supposed to take that pairing?
3. What do you suppose prompted the speaker to draw up his list of "complaints" in the first place? (Is "complaints" the right word?)
4. Do they have any other children? How do you know?
5. How does his wife feel about him? How do you know? How do you feel about them both? Try to communicate how you feel as you read the poem aloud.

2f.   The Licorice Fields at Pontefract

1. What contrasts does the speaker set up between stanzas 1 and 3 and stanza 2? Why do you suppose he does so?
2. Why does he set up the relationship between himself and his "love" as that between a "captive slave" and a "red-haired robber chief"? In what sense is he being over-dramatically humorous (lines 17–18 supporting his description of her in lines 5–8) and also quite bluntly accurate in the long run?

2g. Neutral Tones

1. What is the situation of the poem? Is the speaker talking to someone directly? If not, why does he use "your" in the last three stanzas?
2. Explain the meaning of the images in stanzas 2 and 3. What are the implications of "tedious" (6), "played" (7) and "grin of bitterness" (11)?
3. How do lines 15–16 echo lines 1–4? What is gained by this echoing?
4. In what ways are the implications of the title carried out? Consider word choice, particularly in stanza 1. How do the images of stanzas 2 and 3 emphasize "neutralness"? What is an appropriate synonym for "neutral" in this context: uninvolved? uncommitted? indifferent? lifeless? In what sense is there nothing at all *neutral* about the tone of the poem?
5. How does Hardy, through the extensive use of "and's" in stanzas 1 and 4, reinforce the idea that the dead love affair can be, and constantly is, dredged up from memory? Read the poem giving more than usual emphasis to the "and's" and see what comes out.
6. What are the *keen lessons* to which the speaker refers in stanza 4? In other words, what has the dead love affair come to stand for in his/her life?

3. SOME QUESTIONS ASKED AND ANSWERED

3a. Is My Team Ploughing

1. Who are the speakers in this question and answer session? What do you suppose their relationship was like when the questioner was alive? What is the attitude of the answerer toward the questioner now?
2. What kind of answer does the dead man expect to each of his questions? How is that expectation different from what he gets? Read the poem aloud emphasizing this difference between expectation and actuality. Try it with two different speakers.
3. What difference would there be in what the poem is saying about life and death if the questions were asked in a different order? What importance does the order have to the questioner? to the reader?

3b.   Dinner Guest: Me

1. Characterize the dinner and the conversation. Why does the speaker center so much attention on both?
2. Why was the speaker invited to the dinner party? Why do you suppose he went?
3. What are the actual questions asked here? What are the answers?
4. What are the implied questions asked here? What are the implied answers?

3c.   The Listeners

1. What happens? What is the answer to the Traveler's question: "Is there anybody there?" Who are The Listeners? Why isn't the poem entitled "The Traveler"?
2. Why does the story-teller keep using words like "listening," "hearkening," and "heard" if there are only "phantom listeners" in the house?
3. What do you think the poem is about if it's about more than what literally happens? Does it have to be *about* anything in the usual meaning of the phrase?

3d.   O What Is that Sound

1. Who is asking the questions and who is answering them? Try reading the poem aloud to make clear the characters of the two people as you understand them.
2. When do you suspect that there's more to the "sound which so thrills the ear" than simply the "usual manoeuvres"?
3. What is the effect of the repeated word "dear" at the end of the third line in every stanza but the last? How would you change your saying of the word as the poem progresses? How about the repetitions at the end of each second line?
4. Write a past-tense prose description of what takes place. How is the effect of your prose description different from that of the poem?

3e.   Shall I Wasting in Despair

1. There are some grammatical difficulties here. What punctuation would there normally be in line 1? What does line 19 mean? In lines 27–30 "where" does not refer to "mind," and "want" means

"lack"; therefore, lines 27–28 mean something like, "those of noble mind who find that their wooer is poor. . . ." Thus, "think" is the verb in the sentence. What do the two "them's" refer to? What does "they" in line 29 refer to?

2. What is the effect of the slightly changed repetition of the last two lines in each stanza?
3. What are the two attitudes expressed in lines 35–36 and 37–38?
4. Discuss the validity of the following comments on the poem:

   a. "It's an exercise in sour grapes; the guy must have been jilted."
   b. "It's obvious that the speaker is self-centered and smug."
   c. "The whole thing is a lighthearted spoof of poetry which idolizes women."

3f.   Up-Hill

1. Who is asking the questions? Does the questioner understand the answers? If he (she) does, why does he (she) keep asking questions?
2. Why does the reader take the answers in a different sense from that in which the questioner takes them? When and why does the reader see the questions and answers in a different light?
3. Do you see the poem as simply matter-of-factly ghoulish about dying or as satisfying, if bluntly, reassuring? Why either way? Try reading it to give both impressions. Which do you find easier to do and why?

3g.   Yet Do I Marvel

1. What is the nature of the questions the speaker raises in lines 2–8 that he's sure God could answer about His creation if He wanted to? (If you don't know who Tantalus and Sisyphus are, look them up.)
2. How is the statement in lines 13–14 related to the preceding question? Why isn't it in question form? Or is it? Why does the speaker "marvel"?
3. Does the speaker think that God could "tell why" in answer to the question implied in lines 13–14? Why or why not?
4. How would you characterize the attitude of the speaker: puzzled? flippant? angry? something else? Once you decide, try reading the poem aloud to convey that attitude.

4. SOME ADVICE FREELY GIVEN— AND FREELY IGNORED

4a. When a Man Hath No Freedom to Fight for at Home

1. What advice is the speaker giving here? Does he sound like someone who is suggesting that people behave the way he behaves? Why or why not? Does he believe his own advice?
2. Would you like to have the speaker of the poem fighting for your freedom if you were one of his "neighbors"? Why or why not?
3. Is this the kind of advice that people usually agree with and just as usually ignore? Why?

4b. For Anne Gregory

1. Does the yellow-haired girl prefer having her young men in "despair" regardless of what it is about her that brings on "despair"? Why or why not? What is "despair" in this context?
2. What kind of person is the advice-giver in stanzas one and three? Once you decide what he (she?) is like, read the poem to reveal your feelings about the advice-giver and advice-receiver. Do you think the young girl would really like to be loved for herself alone and not her yellow hair, or that she jolly well likes things the way they are? What do you think the advice-giver thinks? Why is he giving advice? What advice is he giving?

4c. Provide, Provide

1. What specifically does the speaker hope to save the reader from through the advice given? What various ways does he suggest for preventing the worst from happening to one? What does "provide, provide" mean? Do you agree with his assessment of the human predicament? Why or why not?
2. If the advice is serious, why is it given in such flippant, cynical terms? Or aren't the terms flippant and cynical? Or isn't the advice serious? Does it strike you as good advice or bad advice? Does your response tell you something about your own attitude toward preventing what happened to "the beauty Abishag"? What?
3. Once you've decided what the tone of the poem is, try reading it aloud to support that decision.

4d.   Poetry of Departures

1. Why does the speaker find himself "flushed and stirred" (which means what?) by the "epitaphs" heard "fifth-hand" (which means what?)? What does "epitaph" mean here? What does he find appealing about them? Be specific. Do you find them appealing in a similar way? Why or why not? Add a stanza of your own giving a few more similar "fifth-hand epitaphs."
2. Why does the speaker say that acting as the epitaphs suggest would be "artificial . . . a deliberate step backwards"? Why does he get "flushed and stirred" if he knows that what stirs him would be a deliberate step backwards if carried out?
3. What's the advice that is freely given in this poem? In what ways could it be easily ignored?
4. More than in most poems there's the sense here of a person speaking out loud, but probably talking more to himself than to any audience. In reading the poem aloud try to communicate the feeling that the speaker is attracted to what the fifth-hand epitaphs are saying while at the same time rejecting them.

4e.   Underworld

1. What are the "two strange worlds" referred to in line 12? In what sense are they "strange"—to whom? What is the third "strange world" (or the fourth, if Orpheus's hell is the third)? How does one get to that "strange world"?
2. Who is the "you" of line 19? Anybody? Everybody? What advice is being given to the "you"?

4f.   Blue Girls

1. Who are the "blue girls" of the title? Be specific. Why are they called "blue girls"? Is it just because they are wearing blue skirts? (Consider lines 7–8.)
2. In the first three stanzas is the speaker giving advice or simply reporting on what goes on among the blue girls? Why does he speak directly to them—or doesn't he? Determine for yourself what his attitude is and read the poem aloud trying to convey that attitude. (Does he care whether they hear him or not? Does he know whether or not they will pay any attention to him?)
3. What do you gather would be the attitude of the blue girls toward

the advice-giver if they could "hear" it? Can they "hear" it? How do you know?

4g. Sigh No More, Ladies

1. What's the advice in the poem? What do you think of it?

5. SOME SAINTS AND SINNERS

5a. Miniver Cheevy

1. In what sense was Miniver Cheevy the "child of scorn"? In whose eyes? How do you know? What are your own feelings about him?
2. What did Miniver Cheevy want anyway? Do you know any Miniver Cheevy types? What are they like? (They don't have to have ancient historyitis or to have taken up serious drinking.)
3. Once you decide your own attitude toward the Miniver Cheevys of this world, read the poem aloud to convey that attitude.
4. Miniver Cheevy is certainly no saint, but is he a "sinner" in the way the term is used in the phrase "saints and sinners"? Why or why not?

5b. The Gift to Be Simple

1. The poem is about Albert Einstein. What do you know about him? What can you find out?
2. What do the following lines tell about Einstein: 2–3, 4, 5–6, 6–8, 10, 11, 12, 13?
3. Why would it be a "wasted irony" if Einstein were only "remembered for the Bomb"? And why is that remembrance referred to as "such a tomb"?
4. If Einstein was, as so many have said, the father of the atomic bomb, where does that put him on the saint-sinner scale? Where does the speaker put him? What has the poem itself got to do with where you put him?

5c. A Satirical Elegy

1. Swift speaks here of the great Duke of Marlborough, England's

commander-in-chief during the wars against Louis XIV of France. In this light what do lines 6–8 mean? lines 18–24? Who are the "empty things" of line 25?
2. What attitude should the first four lines convey? Read them aloud to give the impression you think is intended. How do the following four support and play off against the first four?
3. What is the tone of the last eight lines? Is it prepared for by what has gone before? Why or why not?
4. In what ways, specifically, was the Duke a "sinner" in the speaker's eyes? Support your answer by specific references to the poem.

5d.   He Was

1. What strengths did the "he" of the poem have? How do you know —what details tell you?
2. "He was all but dumb" means what? "Dumb" in what way? Do you suppose it was because he had nothing to say? Or that he had learned to talk in a different way? The speaker says that he can "now recall / Never a single word / Until . . ."—until what?
3. Where does this man fit along the saint-sinner scale and why? Where would Einstein place him, judging by what the speaker says in the preceding poem?
4. What is the rhyme scheme of the poem? Did you notice that there was a definite pattern before the question was raised? Read the poem aloud, trying purposely to emphasize the rhymes in some sing-song way. Is it possible to do so? Why or why not?
5. This is a memory poem; the speaker is clearly telling of a child-hood remembrance. What does that remembrance now mean to him?

5e.   My Last Duchess

1. This is a dramatic monologue, a one-sided conversation. We know the actions and reactions of the person spoken to only by the in-dications the speaker gives us. We must expect sudden shifts in action without benefit of transitional words or phrases. Point out which of the Duke's comments indicate action or reaction in the emissary he is addressing. Read the poem aloud several times, letting your voice indicate its conversational structure. For one reading, try sympathizing with the Duke's reasons for expecting people to bow and scrape to him.

2. What kind of person was the Duke's *last Duchess?* He refers to her behavior as "this sort of trifling" and says that she *disgusts* him. Just exactly what did she do that disgusted him? How does your response to her behavior differ from the Duke's? Is that because you're not a Duke and therefore don't expect to be kowtowed to? What do you think happened to his last Duchess?

3. What kind of person is the Duke? Refer to specific lines that reveal his attitude toward himself. How does he justify himself according to his standards of conduct? Why does the reader see him differently?

4. How does the Duke's obsession with owning "things" (his art work, for instance) help explain how he could do what he did? Why is the title of the poem particularly appropriate in this connection?

5f.   Unwanted

1. Does the speaker feel sorry for himself? Unhappy? Angry? How would you define his attitude and on what evidence? Try reading the poem aloud to convey the attitude you think he has toward himself.

2. Is it possible that a "poster with [the speaker's] picture on it" could be "hanging on the bulletin board in the Post Office"? Why or why not?

3. What's the nature of his "Warning"? Would you pay any attention to it? Why or why not?

5g.   Reason

1. Characterize the speakers in this curbside drama. How many are there? Where is it taking place? What kind of person is reporting the confrontation?

2. Read the poem aloud, giving the flavor of each participant's comment as it comes across to you. Try doing it with different people speaking the various parts (including that of the reporter).

3. Why do you suppose the "first come, first serve" man reacted the way he did to the other driver's request? Why wasn't the explanation, "I want to unload there" *reason* enough for a reasonable man? Why did he pop out of his car to give the old lady "an elbow" (which means what?)? Why was he all-of-a-sudden being so polite—or wasn't he?

4. The "first come" driver says: "*Reason, reason* is my middle

name." If you don't believe that, what do you think his middle
name is, or should be?

5. What makes the incident amusing and also sobering? Can you
think of a similar sobering one in which your comment on your
behavior could have smugly been, "*Reason, reason* is my middle
name"?

6. SOME NATURAL WAYS OF BEING

6a. The Snow

1. Would you like to be outside during the snowfall described here?
Why or why not? Would it be appropriate to refer to this snowfall
as a "snowstorm" no matter how much snow might get piled up?
What are the connotations of the word "snowstorm"? What are
the connotations of words like "sifts," "powders," "wrinkles,"
"wraps," "flings," "ruffles"?
2. What does the statement "Then stills its artisans like ghosts"
mean? What happens in the last two lines?

6b. Winter Seascape

1. Describe what's going on and compare descriptions with others in
the class. Defend your description with specific references to the
poem. Consider: Which way is the wind blowing? Where is the
speaker standing? Why can he hear the gulls and shags and not
the mongrel hound or little boys? In what sense is the gale a
"cushion" (line 23) and the sea "consoling" (line 24)?
2. Why do you think the speaker refers to himself as "exultant, neutral, free" as he stands on the cliff?
3. In reading the poem aloud pay particular attention to the punctuation and the sound repetitions. What can you say about sound
echoing sense in this poem?

6c. Mushrooms

1. What do the following words mean in context: "Whitely" (line 2):
"Acquire" (line 6); "insist" (line 10)?
2. What do lines 25–29 mean? How about 30–33?
3. What do you now know about mushrooms that you didn't know

before? Do you have any itch to check to see if what the speaker says is true? Did you check? Does it make any difference in what the poem means? What does it mean?

6d.   New Hampshire, February

1. Why do you suppose the speaker "rescued" the two wasps in the first place? He says that he doesn't know why. What is his reference to Michelangelo meant to suggest about him and his motive? What is the comment in line 15 meant to suggest: "While I watched, suspending remarks"?
2. What is the "moral" referred to in line 22? What else is the poem about other than the plight of two ice-cold wasps in New Hampshire in February?

6e.   The Cage

1. How old, in general terms, is the speaker? How is he different, if at all, from the way he was when he saw the caged eagle? What is meant in line 7 by "Love was fiercely caged"? What does the last line of the poem mean?
2. What other kinds of birds are mentioned in the poem and for what purpose? How are they different from the eagle? How does the speaker feel about them?
3. Why did the eagle sit "roosting like a hen on a pole" when "there was room enough" in the cage to fly?
4. Why is the title "The Cage" and not "The Eagle"?
5. The opening line is: "Take, then, this image for what it is worth." What, specifically, is the image the poem deals with? If an image stands for something more than it specifically seems to, what does this one stand for? What is it "worth" to you in both senses?

6f.   Pied Beauty

1. What kinds of things does the speaker want to praise God for? Characterize them. What do all of the things have in common? What do they show about the speaker and the speaker's view of God?
2. Add a few lines of similar things to praise God for. Be as faithful as you can to Hopkins' kind of "beauty."

6g. The Tom-cat

1. Does the speaker like tom-cats? How do you know one way or the other? Or is the question of liking them or not inappropriate here? Why?
2. After deciding what the speaker's attitude towards tom-cats is, read the poem aloud trying to convey that attitude. Try to make your reading imitate the cat's behavior as described by the speaker.